The Queen's Sisters

The lives of the sisters of Elizabeth Woodville

The Queen's Sisters

The lives of the sisters of Elizabeth Woodville

Sarah J. Hodder

Winchester, UK
Washington, USA

JOHN HUNT PUBLISHING

First published by Chronos Books, 2020
Chronos Books is an imprint of John Hunt Publishing Ltd., No. 3 East St., Alresford,
Hampshire SO24 9EE, UK
office@jhpbooks.com
www.johnhuntpublishing.com
www.chronosbooks.com

For distributor details and how to order please visit the 'Ordering' section on our website.

Text copyright: Sarah J. Hodder 2018

ISBN: 978 1 78904 363 1
978 1 78904 364 8 (ebook)
Library of Congress Control Number: 2019939821

A CIP catalogue record for this book is available from the British Library.

Design: Stuart Davies

UK: Printed and bound by CPI Group (UK) Ltd, Croydon, CR0 4YY
US: Printed and bound by Thomson-Shore, 7300 West Joy Road, Dexter, MI 48130

We operate a distinctive and ethical publishing philosophy in
all areas of our business, from our global network of authors to
production and worldwide distribution.

Contents

Acknowledgements

Thanks are due to Christine at St John's Church, Hillingdon, who was so helpful with details of the Lestrange Brass and the manor of Colham. Also, to Craig Irving of Arundel Castle Archives for his assistance with details of the Fitzalan tomb. I am indebted to Amy Licence for her encouragement in the early stages of the book and for reminding me that you are never too old to write! And lastly thanks to my family for allowing me to drag them around castles and manor houses and putting up with my passion for all things historical.

Preface

The Woodville family have, in the most part, received a lot of criticism since Elizabeth, their eldest daughter, became the first commoner to take a giant leap up the social ladder to become Queen of England. The tale of the widower Elizabeth, waiting under an oak tree to speak with the passing Edward IV, only to have him fall in love with her is up there with the best of romances.

But the royal marriage was hugely unpopular from the start and the anti-Woodville propaganda began almost immediately. Described as upstarts and ruthless social climbers, Edward's new and very large extended family were seen to be taking advantage of their new proximity to the king. Even before Elizabeth's coronation, advantageous matches to desirable heirs and heiresses were beginning to be arranged for Elizabeth's siblings, some of which greatly offended the nobility of the realm. In truth Edward IV who would certainly have had to agree, if not suggest these matches, was quite sensibly attempting to keep himself and his crown secure by making as many alliances as possible. This was a time when marriages were very much made to forge allegiances, and by marrying his wife's siblings into important families, Edward achieved a loyal band of supporters which would have been of vital importance during these turbulent times. However, one marriage in particular – the union of the twenty-year-old John Woodville to Katherine Neville, the Dowager Duchess of Norfolk, who was well into her 60s – did little to help dissuade the bad feeling amongst the nobility towards the Woodville family. The marriage was scathingly described by the chronicler, William Worcester, as a 'maritagium diabolicum'[1] and perhaps in hindsight was not the smartest way of endearing his new family to his peers. But there is no evidence that the Dowager Duchess objected to the marriage, and Edward was not in the business of trying to please people. Somewhat ironically, the duchess outlived her young spouse by nearly fifteen years, last being seen at the coronation of Richard III.[2]

Over the centuries that followed, the 'Woodville' clan have been discussed as if they were a single entity, giving the impression that each one of them had designs on climbing the social ladder in search of riches and power. But to judge them as a collective is unjust and unreasonable.

Elizabeth's siblings would, by way of normal human behaviour, have had differing thoughts and emotions about their sister's sudden rise to queenship and about their own arranged marriages that stemmed from this rise into royal circles. For the Woodville men it would have been a huge opportunity to advance themselves, and for John Woodville, married to someone he may have been completely incompatible with, it would have been much easier, as it was much more acceptable, in fact even expected, for men to take mistresses. But for Elizabeth's sisters, as was expected of all women of the period, their role in society was to obtain a good marriage, to look after their husband and to take care of his every need as well as run the household, the estate and of course the most important role of all, motherhood. By reason of probability, we can assume that some of Elizabeth's sisters fared better than others in their new lives but were they, as history suggests, all cut from the same cloth? In truth, like any large family, the Woodvilles were a group of individuals, each with their own personality, thoughts and opinions. Indeed, some of her siblings were still children at the time Elizabeth became queen. For the six-year-old Katherine Woodville and ten-year-old Jane Woodville for instance, it must all have seemed like a huge adventure and it is highly unlikely that they were plotting and planning their way to the upper echelons of society at such a young age.

With the popularity of Elizabeth, 'The White Queen' in

modern fiction, the story of the Woodvilles has reached new audiences. Elizabeth's life has been well-documented and alongside her the fortunes of her parents and male siblings. This brief history concentrates on the females of the family.

Precisely because they were female, they do not feature heavily in the documentary evidence left to us today and sadly their voices, thoughts and emotions are forever lost to us. The earliest historians were men and they wrote about men, if women did feature it was often the briefest of mentions. However, by looking at the few documentary pieces of evidence that do exist concerning these women, the men they married, the families they married into and the places they may have lived, we can piece together a small part of their stories, against a backdrop of the events at the time. With a little imagination we can bring them to life again and gain a tiny glimpse into their worlds. The women of the family, who had much less power than their male counterparts, were likely just normal women of their time, whose sister happened to marry into the royal family, a decision over which they would have had no control, but which irrevocably shaped the course of their lives.

Introduction

Now win who may, ye lusty folk of youth, this garland fresh, of flowers red and white, purple and blue, and colours full uncouth, And I shall crown him king of all delight!

May Day 1464 – as dawn breaks a young woman rises from her bed. Taking care not to disturb the rest of the household, she leaves the house and proceeds to a nearby hermitage. Accompanied only by her mother, she arrives at this pre-arranged destination to find her husband-to-be waiting for her. A short marriage ceremony follows, presided over by a priest and witnessed by her mother and at most two other witnesses, all who have been sworn to secrecy. No pomp, no ceremony, just a dawn meeting of lovers. As the sun rose, and the month of May began, a union was forged that would remain unbreakable for the next nineteen years. And on that early May morning, the young woman changed the fortune and destiny of her family forever. For that woman was Elizabeth Woodville, daughter of Richard Woodville, a lowly knight, and his wife Jacquetta of Luxembourg. And her new husband was Edward IV, King of England.

It was not until September of that year that the marriage was announced publicly. Whether Elizabeth's siblings became aware of their new brother-in-law before then is unknown – maybe the secret was shared with some of her elder or closest siblings? After months of meeting in secret and what must have been an anxious time for Elizabeth, Edward finally announced their union at the council of Reading. He was unable to consider a foreign bride, he declared, as he was already married to the Lady Elizabeth. The announcement was met with shock and disbelief by most of the council. The Earl of Warwick, the 'Kingmaker' who had played a huge role in Edward's journey to the throne, had been in the process of negotiating a French bride for Edward and was furious that he had not been involved in this decision. This could arguably be the point where their relationship started to deteriorate. The Woodvilles were only minor gentry and Edward had been expected to marry a foreign bride, who would have bought with her huge benefits including a large dowry and sealed an alliance with a European power. Elizabeth's marriage bought no benefit to the crown or country and not only was she of questionable class, she was also a widow with two young sons.

Elizabeth's sisters, from hereon in were thrown into a different world, one of pomp and pageantry, husbands and children, political intrigue and court revelry. For Jacquetta, Anne, Margaret, Mary, Jane and Katherine, their sister had catapulted them into the history books as sisters to a queen, and as they grew into womanhood each had to carve a life out for themselves. This book is a brief discussion of their lives.

Note: The dates of births of all of Elizabeth's siblings are often disputed, with different sources giving a variation of birth order and dates. In her book 'The Woodvilles' by Susan Higginbotham, the author evidences a note written in the 1580s by Robert Glover, Somerset Herald (below). It would seem a good fit and a highly possible scenario of the birth order of the Woodville family. It is often debated whether Elizabeth or Anthony was the eldest Woodville child – both were probably born between sometime between 1437 and 1440. John Woodville was described as twenty years old when he married the Dowager Duchess in 1465 and Katherine, as the youngest sibling, has a birth date of around 1458. The other girls fall in between these two dates. For want of any other concrete evidence, this is the order I have followed in this account. (See Appendix One.)

Richard Erle Ryvers and Jaquett Duchesse of Bedford hath

yssue Anthony Erle Ryvers, Richard, Elizabeth first wedded to Sir John Grey, after to Kinge Edward the fourth, Lowys, Richard Erle of Riueres, Sir John Wodeuille Knight, Jaquette lady Straunge of Knokyn, Anne first maryed to the Lord Bourchier sonne and heire to the Erle of Essex, after to the Erle of Kent, Mary wyf to William Erle of Huntingdon, John Woodville, Lyonell Bisshop of Sarum, Margaret Lady Maltravers, Jane Lady Grey of Ruthin, Sir Edward Woodville, Katherine Duchesse of Buckingham.

Note on spelling: I have used the modern version of their surname throughout the book as it is more commonly seen today, but Woodville is not a version they would have recognised in the fifteenth century and was first used in the sixteenth century. Although there are many variants of spellings, the family would likely have used Wydeville, Widville or Widvile.

Chapter One

Jacquetta Woodville, Lady Strange

To do this according to her right she must conduct herself with such wisdom, that she will be both feared and loved

If, as discussed in the previous introduction, we accept Robert Glover's chronology for the birth order of the Woodville siblings, Jacquetta Woodville was most likely born c.1446 as she is named just after John Woodville who was said to have been twenty in 1465, giving him a birth date of 1445. This makes Jacquetta the eldest of Elizabeth's sisters. For Jacquetta and her other siblings, we can only assume that their birthplace was the family manor of Grafton, their country home in Northamptonshire. This is likely to have been the case as their mother, Jacquetta, would most surely have returned home for her confinement, unless circumstances prevented that. When Richard Woodville and his new wife, Jacquetta, returned home from France in late 1436, early 1437 they were in service to the Lancastrian king and queen, Henry VI and Margaret of Anjou. The recently widowed Jacquetta had been married to the Duke of Bedford, the king's uncle, and although the newly married couple made Grafton their home, Jacquetta was often with the queen, serving as one of her ladies, and apparently struck up a good friendship with her. Sir Richard was also often away from home, serving in Calais until 1456 and then being posted to Rochester Castle in 1457. Jacquetta went with him on this posting. It may be, therefore, that some of the Woodville children were born elsewhere. However, Grafton is where they spent their childhood and in the absence of firm evidence, we will assume they were all born in their family home.

After the marriage of their eldest daughter Elizabeth to the

Yorkist king, the process of matching Elizabeth's many siblings with advantageous spouses, the subject of much controversy, began. The young Jacquetta, however, was not part of these proceedings as she was already married and has been since an early age to John Lestrange, 8th Lord Strange of Knockyn.

The Lestrange family (variants of the name are Le Strange, Lestraunge) were an ancient family whose lineage has been traced back to a Roland Lestrange in the 12th century.[1] The name is of French origin and John Lestrange descended from the elder line of the family who titled themselves Lords of The Manor of Knockyn. The pedigree of the Barons of Strange of Knockyn shows that a John Lestrange (V) was first summoned to Parliament on 29th December 1299 as the 1st Lord Strange of Knockyn and the title then passed down through the family.

Jacquetta's chosen spouse was born on 20th May 1444 and was just five years old when he succeeded his father, Richard Lestrange, to the title. An entry in the calendar of patent rolls, dated March 27th 1450, grants the manor of Midlyngton (now known as Middleton Stoney) 'to John Lestraunge and Jacquetta his wife and the heirs of their bodies'.[2] This would indicate that by 1450, Jacquetta was already John's wife – she would have been about four and he about six years old.

Unusually for the second eldest daughter, it seems that Jacquetta's marriage was arranged before her elder sister Elizabeth's. This may be simply due to the proximity in ages of the pair, Elizabeth would have been eight- or nine-years John's senior and therefore may not have been deemed a suitable match. Also, why the marriage was arranged so early, or the connection between the two families, is unclear.

John was the product of his father's second marriage to Elizabeth Cobham in 1439. Richard was already of advanced years when they married (he was the same age as her father!) and Elizabeth was his second wife. His first marriage produced no issue. When Elizabeth gave birth to John, Richard was in his early sixties – he died in 1449 before his only son and heir reached his sixth birthday.[3]

Elizabeth Cobham was the daughter of Sir Reynold Cobham, Knight, (1381 to 1446) and it is a possibility that either Richard Lestrange or Sir Reynold had served in France at some point with the Duke of Bedford. John, Duke of Bedford was, of course, the first husband of Jacquetta's mother, Jacquetta of Luxembourg. With her father, Earl Rivers, also serving in France, perhaps acquaintances were made and that is how a connection between the families came about.

Incidentally, John's mother, Elizabeth, was sister to the infamous Eleanor Cobham, the mistress and then wife of Humphrey, Duke of Gloucester. Humphrey was younger brother to John, Duke of Bedford, and Jacquetta would have known her former sister-in-law. Although tenuous and probably not the connection that led to the marriage of John Lestrange and the younger Jacquetta, it illustrates another family connection to the Cobham family. Eleanor was famously arrested on charges of witchcraft in 1442, accused of commissioning a horoscope that predicted Henry VI would suffer ill health. Witchcraft was an extremely dangerous accusation levelled against women and once made, it was almost impossible to prove your innocence. Eleanor was sentenced, without trial, and her husband, Duke Humphrey, who had once had his first marriage declared unsound so he could marry her when she was his mistress, declared that their union had been bought about by sorcery. Eleanor was forced to do penance, parading through the streets barefoot and in her undergarments to be shamed in front of the gathered crowds, before being imprisoned. She spent the rest of her years incarcerated, dying in 1452.

Whether the terms of the marriage were begun by Richard Lestrange before his death in 1449 or whether it was John's mother Elizabeth who arranged the match for her son, either way the young John and Jacquetta found themselves wed at extremely young ages. This may seem extraordinary to us in the 21st century but was a perfectly normal custom of the time, when alliances between families were forged by the marriage of their children, particularly as marriages nearly always involved a financial settlement. In canon law marriage was legal when the individuals came of age which was usually considered twelve for girls and fourteen for boys. A marriage ceremony could be performed at an earlier age, usually when the child had reached seven or more. However, amongst the nobility the children may have been younger even than this, particularly in situations where the child was an heir or heiress. Jacquetta's future nephew, Richard Duke of York, was married to Anne Mowbray when he was only four years old (and Anne was five) and her youngest sister, Katherine, was married to the Duke of Buckingham at around the ages of seven and ten respectively. The marriage would not be consummated though until it was felt the couple were ready, which again was generally considered to be in their early teens. There are accounts of young girls giving birth at very early ages though, Margaret Beaufort being one such example, who gave birth at the age of thirteen.

An individual would be considered a child until they were seven years old and it was considered both usual and reasonable for children to remain with their mothers up until this age. After this, young girls could be sent to live with the families of their intended grooms (as Elizabeth Woodville herself was when she was sent to live with the Greys at Groby in Leicestershire). In this case, John's only remaining parent, his mother Elizabeth, died only a few years after his father, in 1453, so by the age of ten, John found himself an orphan. His mother had remarried quite quickly after his father's death, to Sir Roger Kynaston. Where John lived after 1453 is unknown, however his stepfather gained the seat of Myddle Castle in Shropshire through the death of John's mother, so perhaps he resided there until he came of age.

Sir Roger Kynaston's military career was as a confirmed

Yorkist and he may have influenced his young stepson in this regard. The eighteen-year-old John was knighted at the coronation of Edward IV in 1461 and was summoned to Parliament from February 28th 1467 to August 19th 1472, with the rolls containing proof of his sitting. He is also named as one of the peers who took the oath of allegiance to Prince Edward in 1471 after Edward reclaimed the throne for the second time and we meet John again in a commission on February 13th 1477 to 'John Straunge of Straunge, knight/ he being named first with sixteen others to inquire by oath into the capture of swans and cygnets on the Thames and its tributaries from Cirencestre to its mouth, by hooks, nets, lyme strynges, and other engines, the alteration and deletion of the marks of swans, and the taking of swans' eggs, and to arrest and imprison the offenders'.[4]

At what age John and Jacquetta took up residence together as man and wife we cannot ascertain, but in September 1462 a licence was issued for 'John, lord le Strange, son and heir of Elizabeth le Strange, deceased, who is nearly of full age, to enter into all his possessions in England and Wales, and the Marches of Wales'.[5] Jacquetta would have been sixteen and perhaps this is when the pair really began their life together.

Whilst John was busy with his duties, we can assume that Jacquetta was involved in looking after the family estates and motherhood as was expected of her. *The Book of Three Virtues*, written by Christine de Pisan (c.1365-c.1430), an outstanding writer of the period, notably because she was female and able to support herself and family through her writing, gives advice to Baronesses. She acknowledges 'certain barons have enormous power because of their lands, domains, and the nobility that goes with them' and goes on to say their wives 'must be highly knowledgeable about government, and wise – in fact, far wiser than most other such women in power'. She continues, 'If Barons wish to be honoured as they deserve, they spend very little time in their manors and on their own lands. Going to war, attending their prince's court, and travelling are the three primary duties of such a lord. So, the lady, his companion, must represent him at home during his absences. Although her husband is served by bailiffs, provosts, rent collectors, and land governors, she must govern them all. To do this according to her right she must conduct herself with such wisdom that she will be both feared and loved'.[6]

Although Jacquetta had in all possibility never read this advice, this is almost certainly the life she would have been leading. She would have resided at home whilst her husband was away, although due to her family's elevated status, she would also likely have attended at least some royal occasions. If Jacquetta had left home by 1462, which is certainly likely, she would not have been resident at Grafton during the events of 1464. Was it by letter that she was informed of her sister's marriage and elevation to queenship or did a family member ride post haste to break the news? Maybe on hearing, she immediately took a trip back to Grafton to hear the news first-hand or perhaps the first time she got to congratulate her sister was just before her coronation? Even though Jacquetta was a remote step away from the action, 1464 and 1465 would still have been a hugely important time for her.

As well as running her estates, Jacquetta was also a mother. The couple had one surviving daughter, Joan Lestrange born in 1463 when Jacquetta would have been about 17 years old (this may tie in with the assumption that Jacquetta and John may have taken up residence together a year earlier in 1462). Whether there were other pregnancies that didn't go full term or other children that died at an early age is not recorded.

The Lestranges owned many properties that they may have spent time in, including Knockyn Castle and Mydlington in Oxford, neither of which survive today. But it is believed that their main residence may well have been at Colham in Hillingdon, Middlesex.

The manor of Colham entered the Lestrange family in 1331 when it was granted to Eubolo Lestrange and his heirs.[7] In her book *Hillingdon Through Eleven Centuries* (1926), Rachel de Salis tells us that the Lestrange family were soldiers and statesmen and therefore didn't often visit Colham after they acquired it in the fourteenth century and that by 1449 the Manor House was said to be beyond repair. She does however conclude that a Manor House standing on the banks of the Colne, almost equidistant between Windsor and London would be the perfect residence for a nobleman attendant at court

In his itinerary of 1536, Leland gives an account of Colham as standing about a mile above a bridge under which the river Colne runs. We have a record of Richard Lestrange, being assessed at 6s. 8d. towards the subsidy of 1428 in respect of a knight's fee at Coleham (sic), Middlesex, for the campaign in France against Joan of Arc.[8] Perhaps by his death in 1449 the manor had gone into disrepair.

However, it had either been renovated or a replacement Manor House had been built by 1521, as Thomas Earl of Derby (John and Jacquetta's grandson) died there in that year. John Lestrange himself was buried in St John's church in Hillingdon, as was their daughter Joan, so it is not a huge leap to assume that he himself had been living at Colham at the time. Perhaps, it was John and Jacquetta who undertook the renovations and made this their home, perfect for John to travel up to court when required, and after 1464 perfect for Jacquetta to visit her royal sister at Windsor whenever she was in residence. Their daughter, Joan, would likely then have been bought up here.

Several sources claim that Jacquetta is also buried in the church at Hillingdon, but documentary evidence does not support that. When Jacquetta died or where she is interred, is sadly once again not documented, but we do know that she pre-deceased her husband. The first piece of evidence to support this can be found in the patent rolls after John's death, on 26th

February 1480-81 where a statement allows that George Stanley (Joan's husband) and Jane (sic) Lestrange his wife enter into the property late of the said John *'which should descend to her on his death, and after the death of Anne, late the wife of the said John... '*.[9]

Even by a good stretch of the imagination, Anne cannot be a misspelling of Jacquetta, and therefore we must assume that as John had re-married, Jacquetta must have died before him. The other piece of evidence that supports an alternative resting place for Jacquetta is Joan's request in her will to be buried 'by my lorde my ffader in the same tombe'.[10] She also made provisions for three priests to sing, read and pray for her father and mother, her husband and herself for a period of 20 years. Although this is not conclusive evidence that Jacquetta is not buried at Hillingdon, the fact that Joan does not request to be buried alongside her father *and* *mother* would seem to indicate that Jacquetta's resting place is elsewhere.

Jacquetta is still commemorated at Hillingdon, however, in the beautiful Lestrange brass. The brass was commissioned by their daughter Joan in 1509 and is considered to be one of the finest brasses in Middlesex. The slab was originally situated on a chest tomb until the restoration of the church in the 1840s. The Latin inscription on the tomb reads:

Under this tomb lies the noble John Lord L'Estrange, Lord of Knocking, Mohun, Wassett, Warnell and Lacey and Lord of Colham; with a portrait of Janet (sic) at one time his wife, which same Janet was sister to Elizabeth, Queen of England at that time wife of Edward IV; which same John died the 15th day of October in the 17th year of the reign of Edward IV; this tomb Jane, Lady L'Estrange caused to be made with the portrait of Janet at her own expense 1509.[11]

The brass is 6 feet high and 31 inches wide on a marble slab. Lord Strange is featured in armour with a bare head. Jacquetta is wearing a waisted dress, tied with a loosely hanging decorated girdle. An outer gown is open in the front, fastened across the chest by a band decorated with roses. She is wearing a plain headdress. Both are standing under a double canopy and between them is a small effigy of Joan.

So, when did Jacquetta die? John Lestrange died in 1479 and the fact that he remarried means that in all likelihood, Jacquetta had died by 1478 at the latest. Joan was born in 1463 and a possible scenario is that Jacquetta died after giving birth, as was the fate of so many women in this era when childbirth was a dangerous undertaking. The image of the family of three represented on the brass portrays a loving little family and had she been raised by her father and his second wife Anne, she may have seen Anne as the maternal figure in her life. Her wish to have both her mother and father commemorated in this way indicates that perhaps they did get to spend some time together as a family.

Without facts, we can only speculate, but a possible clue could be found at Haughmond Abbey in Shropshire. The Abbey was given its status in the 12th century and its founders were the Fitzalan family. But the Knockyn branch of the Lestrange family were also important benefactors. On December 1st, 1476, John Lestrange made an endowment to the abbey for a perpetual chantry there with daily masses to be said at the altar of St Anne for his and Jacquetta's souls, along with the souls of his parents.[12] A chantry was a fund set up for the purpose of employing a priest (or several priests) to sing a stipulated number of masses for the soul of a deceased person for a specified amount of time. It was believed that these masses would hasten the souls of the deceased person through purgatory and into heaven. Donors of these chantry were very often the deceased person themselves who would leave specifications in their will. Was this endowment made by John in 1476 prompted by the fact that he had been recently bereaved? This was thirteen years before John himself died which would have been enough time for him to have sought a second wife. Sadly, without further evidence, we will never know if this is the case but if Jacquetta did die in 1476, she would have been around thirty years of age. She would have lived long enough to see her sister flee into sanctuary in 1470, lived through the deaths of both her parents but not survived to witness the death of Edward IV and the chaotic events that followed.

Her daughter Joan, however, did live through the turbulent times after Edward's death and as with many women, was personally affected as events played out. When John died, Joan succeeded him as 9th Baroness of Knockyn. Joan was married by 1481 to George Stanley, the son of Thomas, Lord Stanley, one of the famous Stanley brothers who are credited with helping Henry Tudor win the Battle of Bosworth and take the crown. In right of his wife, George was summoned to parliament as a Baron during his father's lifetime. After the Battle of Bosworth, Thomas Stanley was made Earl of Derby by Henry VII.

The Stanleys were notorious for remaining neutral for as long as possible and not picking a side until they were sure who would be the victor. This was a shrewd move and ensured their means of survival but in 1485 it nearly cost Joan's husband his life. In the summer of that year, rumours were abounding that Henry Tudor was on his way from exile in France to claim his right to the throne. His mother was Margaret Beaufort and Henry was considered the last hope for the Lancastrians. George's father, Thomas Stanley, was Margaret's husband and in July 1485, no doubt sensing trouble, he excused himself from court to go and visit relatives. Richard III allowed this on the understanding that his son, George, took his place at court. The official reason was that George needed to deputise in his father's absence, but he was more or less held 'hostage' as Richard feared (quite rightly in fact) that Lord Stanley would be persuaded by Margaret to pledge allegiance to her son.

By August 1485 Henry Tudor had landed and the two armies met at Bosworth field. The outcome of the battle is well-known

– the Stanley brothers entered the fray at the last moment on the side of Henry Tudor and it was Lord Thomas Stanley who is reported to have 'crowned' Henry on the battlefield. Before fighting began, Richard III ordered Thomas Stanley and his brother to take their positions with his men. Henry Tudor was also requesting their presence, but the brothers delayed taking action, leaving both Henry and Richard unsure of their allegiance. Richard, furious at their hesitation, ordered that George be executed. For whatever reason, this order wasn't carried out and George managed to escape death and survived the Battle of Bosworth to fight another day.

Although not privy to events on the battlefield, Joan would have likely been aware her husband was to all intents and purposes being held hostage and this must have been a frightening time for her. Joan and George went on to become parents of four sons and three daughters, Jacquetta's grandchildren. George died before his father in 1503, allegedly of poison, and Joan died in 1513 and was buried at Hillingdon with her father. Their eldest son, Thomas, became the second Earl of Derby on his grandfather's death and inherited the barony of Knockyn on his mother's side which was merged into the earldom.

Jacquetta is not mentioned by name in many of the sources concerning the reign of her sister and Edward IV and it is tempting to wonder if her shadowy existence means she may have managed to live a life least touched by the trappings of court life and politics. She cannot have been in love with her husband at the time of her betrothal, in all likelihood they had never even met, but they hopefully managed to forge a life together that contained some happiness. Perhaps the second eldest daughter of Richard and Jacquetta Rivers managed to strike the best balance out of all her siblings by leading her life on the periphery of events, whilst being able to join her family for times of celebration.

Chapter Two

Anne Woodville, Lady Bourchier

The most splendid court that could be found in all Christendom

Anne was the third Woodville daughter born to Richard and Jacquetta, again most likely at Grafton sometime around 1447. Unlike her two elder sisters, Elizabeth and Jacquetta, it does not appear that any arrangements for a marriage for Anne were in place before Elizabeth became Queen of England or if discussions had started, they are unknown and were presumably disregarded. So, it was in or around February 1466 that the nineteen-year-old Anne found herself wed to William Bourchier, a cousin and close ally of the king.

William's mother, Isabel of Cambridge, was the elder sister of Richard Plantagenet, Duke of York, and thus Edward's aunt. Her husband, William's father, was Henry Bourchier. Henry was a military man to the core and had seen considerable military action in France, serving under the Duke of York during the reign of Henry VI. He had been created a Viscount during the 1445-6 parliament and on 30th June 1461 he was created Earl of Essex by Edward IV after fighting alongside the Yorkists in the battles of Towton and the second battle of St Albans.

With the whole Woodville family present to celebrate Elizabeth's coronation in 1465, Anne then became the only sister to afterwards join Elizabeth at court. Perhaps she had the closest relationship with her elder sister, even with the nine- or ten-year age gap between the two, or perhaps William was at court and it was therefore deemed appropriate for Anne to remain there too, taking up a place as one of Elizabeth's ladies. This position earned her a salary of £40 a year, detailed in Elizabeth's only surviving household accounts from 1466-67:

Et Anne, Domine Bourgchier, Elizabeth, Domine Scales,1 attendentibus circa personam domine regine, videlicet utrique earum, pro feodo suo hoc anno, £40...[1]

Not a huge amount is known about William Bourchier, including his date of birth. His parents were married sometime around 1426, and as William was their eldest son he could have been born as early as 1427-28, which would have made him almost twenty years older than Anne. William and Edward were cousins, although Edward was not born until 1444 so they may not have been close childhood playmates if William was indeed into his teens when Edward was born. As the elder member of the Bourchier family, it was William's father, Henry, who held the more senior positions at court, serving at various times as Lord Treasurer, Steward of the Household, Keeper of the King's Great Seal and Master of the King's Hounds.[2] With Anne residing at court, it was likely that William did too, perhaps serving Edward in a more minor position in his household.

Between 1466-1469 life at court would have been a new and exciting time for the newlyweds. The new royal family also settled into life and Elizabeth excelled at her queenly duties, quickly producing three children, Elizabeth in 1466, Mary in 1467 and Cecily in 1469. With their first three offspring all being female, the longed-for birth of a son and heir was not immediately forthcoming, but Elizabeth was proving herself strong and fertile and there would have been hope that a son would soon follow. But underneath this picture of domesticity, there were rumblings. The Earl of Warwick and Edward IV had been on a collision course for a while – the Earl, his former mentor and 'Kingmaker' had strongly disapproved of Edward's marriage and now as king, Edward was not proving to be as pliable as perhaps Warwick had hoped he would be. Edward's brother George, Duke of Clarence, was also making trouble whenever he could and when Edward refused to allow George to be married to Warwick's eldest daughter, Isabel Neville, the pair went ahead and married anyway on 11th July 1469. But this was no love match, it had been engineered by the Earl as a path to the throne. With Edward out of the way, (although they may have been unsure at this stage how exactly they were going to make that happen), George would be next in line to be king (as Edward was yet to produce a son), with Warwick's daughter as his queen.

The year 1469 saw uprisings and skirmishes and in a horrific turn of events for the Woodville family, Earl Rivers and John Woodville (Anne's father and brother) were captured and beheaded by the Duke of Clarence and Earl of Warwick. Accounts tell of the sadness this would have bought to the queen and her mother Jacquetta, but Anne Woodville would have been equally shocked and upset at this news. Like the rest of the court, she must have felt incredibly unsettled, trying to support her sister, the queen, whilst dealing with her own emotions. For his next move, Warwick made a hapless attempt at taking control of the king. Both these events took place in the aftermath of the Yorkist defeat at the Battle of Edgecote. Edward who had ridden north to deal with the uprisings, found himself without an army (who had all fled) and alone with just a handful of supporters. He was captured at Olney and taken to Warwick Castle. However, without a firm plan, of how to dispose of the king, it seemed that the Earl could not raise enough supporters to remove Edward from the throne. Without their king, the country descended into chaos and Warwick found himself unable to regain control. He also could not bring himself to actually commit cold-blooded murder of his king at this time and he embarrassingly had to let Edward go. Edward returned to London at the end of 1469 and the court spent Christmas at Westminster; Anne would certainly have hoped the yuletide festivities would now herald a peaceful new year.

Edward's court was already lauded as splendid, but Christmas and New Year festivities would have bought with them the chance for Anne and William to dress in their finery and perhaps to relax a little in their duties to enjoy the season. Describing a later court Christmas of 1482 (which was unknowingly to be the king's last), the writer of the Croyland Chronicle remarks that the royal court presented an appearance that 'fully befits a most mighty kingdom, filled with riches and boasting of those sweet and beautiful children, the issue of his marriage with Queen Elizabeth'.[3] In 1469, there were only three royal children, but no doubt Christmas at Westminster would have been a glorious affair.

But 1470 did not bring peace, and although the earl and duke were down, they were certainly not out. September of that year heralded the 'end' of Edward's first term as King of England. Warwick and Clarence had become strong enough to threaten real danger to the king and Edward found himself with little choice but to flee to France, along with his younger brother Richard of Gloucester, and a loyal retinue of up to 800 men.[4] Quite likely at least one of the Bourchier men may have accompanied him, if not both. A heavily pregnant Elizabeth, realising that her life may be in danger, fled into the sanctuary of Westminster Abbey along with her mother and daughters. As for Anne, as one of Elizabeth's ladies, this must have been a frankly worrying time. Evidence of Anne's whereabouts during this time is unclear. She may have remained at court, particularly if her husband had accompanied Edward abroad, and may even have been a go-between, taking her sister and mother news in sanctuary whenever she could. With Edward out of the way, Warwick and Clarence re-instated the hapless Henry VI, although essentially, he was just a puppet king under Warwick's control. If Anne did remain, she would have had to have kept her head down and tried to exude an air of neutrality in the service of the Lancastrian king. Or she perhaps retired, either with or without her husband, to one of their properties, away from the immediate danger to watch and await the outcome.

The re-instated Lancastrian Government paid Elizabeth, Lady Scrope, £10 to attend the queen in sanctuary[5], and Anne may have been able to send communication via her, or even attend the queen herself on occasions. If she did, she may have assisted her sister in the birth of her first son, also named Edward, who was born in sanctuary on 2nd November 1470. It would have been a mixed occasion of joy at the birth of a son, the longed-for Yorkist Prince, and sadness at the situation that the Woodville family now found themselves in.

After a long six months in exile, Edward and his supporters returned to England to reclaim his throne and on 14th April 1471 the Battle of Barnet took place, followed in quick succession by the Battle of Tewkesbury. William Bourchier was present at Barnet (erroneously noted by some sources to have been killed in the battle), and presumably William and his father were also part of Edward's forces in Tewkesbury. During the Battle of Barnet, the Earl of Warwick was killed. The Battle of Tewkesbury then saw the capture of Henry VI's queen, Margaret of Anjou, who herself had returned from exile in France, and the death of her only son, Edward, thus removing the Lancastrian threat once and for all. Also taken from near the battlefield at Tewkesbury was the Earl of Warwick's younger daughter, Anne Neville, who had been hastily married to the Lancastrian heir, Edward, in France. She had been her father's back-up plan as he had begun to realise that George, Duke of Clarence and his eldest daughter were not likely to be able to take the throne from Edward. Ironically, Anne did eventually go on to achieve queen status, as the wife of Richard III, but Warwick did not live long enough to witness that.

Edward had triumphed and returned once again to London to reclaim his throne. A few days after his return, the re-captured Lancastrian king, Henry VI, died in the tower, supposedly of natural causes. At least that was the official statement! Edward and Elizabeth's newborn son, Edward, was created Prince of Wales and the king and queen also took part in a second coronation at Westminster on Christmas day and twelfth night.[6] We can assume that if Anne chose to return to royal service, she would have taken part in the celebrations. Finally, the king and queen could feel secure on their thrones, their opponents were either dead or had fled abroad, and they could finally look forward to a more calm and secure future.

So, with 1471 seeing the beginning of Edward's second reign, the court once again resumed normal business. The court of Edward and Elizabeth was modelled on the magnificence of the Burgundian court and Anne and William would no doubt also have lived in comparative luxury. Although Edward and Elizabeth's courts were run as separate entities, the two households would have come together often to dine and to spend their leisure time.

In 1472 a good friend of Edward's, Louis de Gruuthuyse, visited England and the description of the visit paints a splendid picture of the court at play. Louis was Governor of Holland, under Charles the Bold, and had sheltered Edward during his time in exile. He was visiting England in order to be created Earl of Winchester and stayed at Windsor with the Royal Family as an honoured friend. During his time at court Louis was entertained in Elizabeth's apartments where she was playing bowls with her ladies – it is highly likely that Anne was amongst this group of ladies. Amy Licence in her book *Edward IV and Elizabeth Woodville*, describes how Louis witnessed apartments richly hung with white silk and linen and cloths of arras, and beds that were draped with fine French sheets, canopies and counterpanes of cloth of gold and ermine. Anne and William's apartments would not have been quite this luxurious, but they certainly would have led a comfortable life as part of this rich and vibrant court.

During their marriage, Anne and William had three children:

Henry, Cecily and Isabel. As a mother, Anne could have chosen to remain at court serving her sister. Indeed, juggling motherhood and court duties was a familiar scenario for many ladies such as the mother of another future queen, Elizabeth Boleyn, who half a century later divided her time between raising her children at Hever Castle and attending court to perform her duties in the household of Katherine of Aragon. Her mother, Jacquetta, had also had several pregnancies during her time in service to Queen Margaret. Anne may have chosen to do the same, retiring to the Bourchier estates during her confinement and childbirth and then returning to court to resume her duties once she had been churched.

Their son and heir, Henry Bourchier, also chose a military career, following in the footsteps of his father and grandfather. He served as a soldier in the courts of both Henry VII and Henry VIII and inherited the title Earl of Essex on the death of his grandfather. The senior Henry (William' father), was a robust fellow and William pre-deceased him and therefore never acquired the title Earl of Essex, which passed after Henry's death to his grandson. Anne therefore never found herself Countess of Essex.

The younger Henry was first cousin to Henry VII's queen, Elizabeth, and served as a member of Henry's Privy Council. He married twice but only had one daughter with his first wife, Mary Saye. Their daughter was named Anne, probably after her grandmother, Anne Woodville. Anne's namesake went on to cause quite a furore in her lifetime when she had an affair and eloped with her lover. Her cuckolded husband was William Parr, brother of Queen Katherine Parr. Having been married to her husband at the age of ten, the couple were by all accounts unhappy from the start and today we would likely have more sympathy for Anne's predicament but in the sixteenth century her behaviour was considered scandalous.

Little is known about Cecily Bourchier apart from her marriage to John Devereux, earning herself the title Baroness Ferrers. The couple reportedly had two surviving children, Walter and Ann Devereux. Cecily died in 1493.

Isabel Bourchier remained unmarried, which was unusual for a fifteenth century female. Many unmarried women at the time took holy orders and joined a nunnery but Isabel did not choose that as her vocation. The unmarried Lady Isabel Bourchier died in 1501, leaving her brother, Henry, half the £200 that their paternal grandmother had left her.[7] Before her demise Isabel boarded out and perhaps used her dowry to support herself as was often the case. Isabel was recorded as living in London, boarding with a John Halhed and his wife Gertrude. In her will she left items to both John and Gertrude and their servant, Katherine Birche, and asked to be buried with her sister, Cecily.[8]

William Bourchier died in early 1483. He was alive apparently in February of that year when he was made a commissioner of the peace[9] but had died before April 1483, which was when his father died, and the Earldom passed directly to Henry, Anne and William's son. His place of burial is unknown, but his father was originally buried at Beeston Abbey, before being re-interred in the Bourchier chapel at Little Easton at the time of the dissolution of the monasteries. Little Easton Manor House was home to Henry and Isabel, and Edward IV and Elizabeth are rumoured to have honeymooned there in 1464. The estate passed into the younger Henry's ownership after his grandfather's death. William and Anne may never have lived there, if they resided mainly at court, although perhaps it is a property Anne may have known and maybe where she gave birth to her three children? Given the short timing between the death of both father and son, perhaps William was also buried at the Abbey or in Little Easton.

After William's death, Anne remarried, although there is some confusion over dates and indeed husbands! Several sources indicate she took as her second husband a gentleman called Edward Wingfield. However, there is no doubt that she also married George Grey, 5th Lord Grey of Ruthin and eventual 2nd Earl of Kent. George was a younger brother to Anthony Grey, Lord Grey of Ruthin, who had married her sister Jane (see chapter five). There doesn't appear to be much time for Anne to have married Edward, particularly as he outlived her, so she would have had to have divorced him to marry George Grey. There is some evidence that Edward Wingfield may have been her sister Jane's second husband and again this is discussed in the later chapter on Jane.

We do know that Anne married George Grey in or after 1483.[10] George Grey was the second son, and styled Lord Grey of Ruthin after the death of his older brother Anthony. He eventually succeeded to the Earldom of Kent after the death of his father, but this did not occur during Anne's lifetime, and so although she had been married into two aristocratic families, Anne never achieved the title of Countess of either Essex or Kent!

The couple had one son Richard, 6th Lord Grey, who eventually became the 3rd Earl of Kent. However, dates given for Richard's birth are somewhat confusing, with several sources citing his birth date before his parents were married. He was allegedly twenty-five in 1503, placing his birth date in 1478.[11] Other sources give his birth date as 1481. There is always the possibility that William Bourchier died earlier than 1483, and that Anne and George married before 1478. It is likely that they may have already known each other as their siblings had been married since the mid-1460s and their paths would no doubt have crossed. Perhaps there was a long-lasting attraction to each other that they had tried to ignore over the years until such time as they were both free? As tempting as it is to hope this was a marriage made for love, it cannot also be discounted of course, that this second marriage was also arranged by the king and queen. The couple were certainly closer in age than Anne was with her previous husband, with Anne being perhaps six or seven years older, so maybe Anne was able to choose her second husband. It is also tempting to wonder whether the couple conceived before they were married, perhaps not in William's lifetime, which would have caused quite a scandal, but the dates are very confusing and leave more questions than answers!

With Edward IV's death in 1483, there is no record of Anne remaining at court to serve Anne Neville, Queen of Richard III. She may have chosen to leave court (indeed if she did serve her sister throughout the entirety of her reign and hadn't left already) and move to one of her husband's residences, perhaps Ampthill, the favoured residence of the De Grey family (see the chapter on Jane).

George Grey made several appearances in the records, including fighting alongside Henry in the Battle of Stoke in June 1487. A Lady Grey de Ruthyn was in attendance at Prince Arthur's christening in 1486 and also mentioned as part of the celebrations for Elizabeth of York's coronation in 1487, although this could also again refer to her sister, Jane, who was the widowed Lady Grey de Ruthin at this time. Whomever the reference refers to though, it is hugely possible that both sisters were there supporting their niece.

Anne died in July 1489, aged around forty-two and was buried in the church of Warden Abbey, Bedfordshire. Her husband, George, did remarry but died in 1503 at Ampthill and was also buried at Warden Abbey, presumably alongside Anne. Having spent a good part of her life at court, Anne was probably the one whose life was most closely entwined with her sister Elizabeth's, and she witnessed more than any of the others, life at the most celebrated court in Christendom!

Chapter Three

Mary Woodville, Countess of Pembroke

Not farre from thence, a famous Castle fine, That Ragland hight, stands moted almost round...the Fountaine trim, that runs both day and night, Doth yield in showe, a rare and noble sight.

Between 1446 when Jacquetta Woodville was born and 1453 when their brother Lionel was born, there is a gap of seven years. Anne was the next sibling to be born after Jacquetta, so we can assume a birth date for her of 1447 at the earliest. Mary was next in line after Anne. Robert Glover also lists a son named John, who followed Mary's birth and who presumably didn't survive to adulthood. Again, simple maths tells us that unless he was a twin, John must have been born by 1452 at the latest, which places Mary Woodville's birth date sometime between 1447 and 1451.

The young Mary was born into an ever-expanding family, with her parents riding high in the favour of the Lancastrian king and queen, Henry VI and Margaret of Anjou. Around the time of her birth in 1448 her father was awarded a promotion by the king to baron, choosing for himself the name Baron Rivers. As one sister was born into the Woodville household, another was preparing to start a family of her own as it was likely around this time that her elder sister Elizabeth's first marriage took place to Sir John Grey of Groby.

Over a decade later, with their daughter Elizabeth now the new Yorkist Queen of England, Mary's parents would attend her own marriage which took place at Windsor Castle in September 1466. Her husband was the Earl of Pembroke's eldest son, William. Various ages are given for William at the time of his marriage. He was noted as being 14 in 1469, (upon the death of his father), giving him a birth date of 1458 and therefore aged eleven at the time of his marriage and other sources claim he was only five when he was betrothed to Mary[1], placing his birth date in 1461. Other references refer to a birth date of 1451 which is more likely to be the case and puts him in the same age bracket as Mary, and in his mid-teens at the time of his wedding. In early September and prior to his wedding ceremony, William had been knighted by the king at Windsor, and given the title Lord Dunster.

William's father, also named William, was a very powerful Welsh magnate. The son of Sir William ap Thomas of Raglan Castle, William senior was a staunch Yorkist with a huge power base covering most of Wales. In the 1450s he had served as the Earl of Warwick's Sheriff of Glamorgan and as steward and constable for the Duke of York's marcher lands.[2] Regarded by his countrymen as a national hero, it was William who had been responsible for running military operations in Wales against the Lancastrians and the loyalty he was shown by his countrymen greatly impeded Jasper Tudor's efforts to raise the men of Wales to fight for the Lancastrian cause. As a reward for his loyalty, he was created Baron Herbert of Raglan in 1461 and made a Knight of the Garter in 1462. His greatest honour came in 1468 when he became the first member of the Welsh Gentry to enter the English Peerage when Edward IV created him Earl of Pembroke.[3]

His importance to the Yorkist dynasty saw him amass considerable wealth and throughout the 1460s, William senior extended and rebuilt Raglan Castle, creating a magnificent residence for his family. Mary would have joined this household in 1466. Her mother-in-law, Anne Devereux was by all accounts a kindly woman, a view that was endorsed by a later King of England, Henry Tudor, who had been bought up in Raglan Castle under her care. In 1455 a twelve-year-old Margaret Beaufort, Henry's mother, had married the twenty-four-year-old Edmund Tudor, half-brother to King Henry VI. Shockingly even by fifteenth century standards, Edmund decided not to wait until his young bride was old enough to consummate the marriage and consequently by spring 1456 Margaret had become pregnant. During her pregnancy, Edmund was captured by William Herbert and imprisoned in Carmarthen Castle, where he subsequently died of the plague. Young and alone in Wales, Margaret sought the protection of her brother-in-law Jasper Tudor at his home, Pembroke Castle, and in January 1457 she gave birth, which due to her young age and small frame was a horrific experience for her. Formidable even from a young age, Margaret left her son in Jasper's care, a few short months after giving birth, and travelled back to England, pluckily arranging a second marriage for herself to safeguard hers and her son's future. However, with the overthrow of the Lancastrian regime in 1461, Jasper Tudor had to flee, seeking exile in France and during a raid of Pembroke Castle, William Herbert discovered the four-year-old Henry Tudor. The new King Edward agreed to sell the young boy's wardship to William Herbert for £1000, a huge sum of money, and Henry was taken to Raglan Castle where he was cared for and remained for eight years. He would later recall his time at Raglan with affection and when he became king in 1485, he invited Ann Devereux to London to visit him at court.[4]

Arriving at Raglan in 1466, the teenage Mary would have had the company of her new husband's extensive family as William had two younger brothers, Walter and George, and six sisters, Maud, Katherine, Anne, Margaret, Cecily and Elizabeth.[5] Coming from a large and bustling household herself, this may have helped Mary settle into her new life in Wales. Mary would also of course have met Henry Tudor, who resided at Raglan until 1469, although it is only in hindsight that we know him as the future Henry VII. To Mary he would simply have been another boy of the household. In September 1467 Mary may also have met Margaret Beaufort and her husband, who travelled to Raglan to visit her son, remaining there for a week and no doubt lavishly entertained by the Herberts in Raglan's 'hundred rooms, filled with festive fare'.[6]

The remains of Mary's marital home, Raglan Castle, are still magnificent today and its impressive form can be seen for miles around the countryside. On arriving in Raglan in 1466, she would first have entered the castle through the impressive gatehouse which in Mary's time was approached by a drawbridge. The drawbridge was replaced by an arch bridge in the sixteenth century. The castle had two courtyards: The Pitched Stone Court which was the domain of the household staff, containing an office wing, and a kitchen block with two large fireplaces and The Fountain Court. The Fountain Court was surrounded by two blocks of guest apartments reached by a grand staircase, a third block of apartments for use by the Earl and his family which overlooked the moat and a set of state apartments which also had a view across the moat. Each chamber was equipped with a fireplace, window seats and access to private latrines. The Fountain Court was probably not known as that when Mary lived there as the fountain it was named after is thought to be late Tudor in date.[7]

The castle also boasted a great hall, no doubt where Margaret Beaufort was entertained in 1467, and its most impressive feature, the three towers. The Great Tower or Yellow Tower of Gwent, largely destroyed during the English Civil War, was the most predominant feature of the castle and along with its two other towers, the Closet and Kitchen Towers, gave a formidable warning to any potential attackers. The buildings were surrounded by orchards and kitchen gardens which were themselves surrounded by extensive parkland.

In 1468, two years after their marriage, William travelled to London to study at Lincoln's Inn. Lincoln's Inn was one of the Inns of Court that gave students an education in English law. A knowledge of law would prove an asset to sons of the nobility, greatly assisting them with the managements of large estates. The Black Books of Lincoln's Inn have records dating back to 1422 and confirm that in September 1468 (8 Edw. IV) 'William Herbert, son of the Earl of Pembroke, adm. at Michaelmas'.[8] Had he been born in or around 1451, William would have been about 17. A birth date of 1461 and even 1458 can almost certainly be discounted. There were no set ages for entrance to university education as we have in the modern world, but seven or ten years of age seems slightly too young for him to enter one of the Inns.

Whilst William was away in London, Mary would have resided with her new family at Raglan, possibly taking the opportunity to visit her husband in London and maybe other members of the Woodville family on occasion. Records of the castle give us a small insight into domestic life with details of the purchase of buckram (cotton or linen fabric) and satin for the females appearing in accounts, as well as a quantity of cloth for livery.[9] Events took a shocking turn for the Herbert family though when in July 1469 her father in law, the Duke of Pembroke and his brother were captured and executed by Warwick and the Duke of Clarence after the Battle of Edgecote. This must have been a terrible time for Mary and her family, first when the news of the death of her father-in-law came through, followed by the awful news that her father and brother John had also met the same violent end. William may have been in London when news was received so this may have been a lonely time for Mary, far away from other members of her family. Records show that the twelve-year-old Henry Tudor was also present at Edgecote as part of the Yorkist forces as he was reportedly led to safety by Sir Roger Corbet and taken to Weobley in Herefordshire, the home of Anne's brother Walter Devereux. It seems that Anne was also present at Weobley at this time, possibly having accompanied her husband on his travels, and the grieving widow continued to look after the young boy for several weeks. Mary, at Raglan, presumably now in charge of her own household, must have felt desperately alone.

In his will written before he went off to battle in mid-July, William appointed Anne as one of his executors and implored her 'to take the mantle and the ring and live a widow'. On the morning of his execution he added a codicil saying: 'and wife that you remember your promise to me to take the order of widowhood, as you may be the better master of your own to perform my will and help my children, as I love and trust you'. As a father of several illegitimate children, it seems a bit extreme from a modern viewpoint for the Earl to specify that his wife should not remarry. However, apart from the romantic viewpoint that it might have indicated a great love between Earl William and his wife, in a practical sense it was also a safeguard to ensure that the Herbert estates remained under the control of Anne and her family. Widows in medieval times were able to run their own estates and take care of their children but once they remarried, their power completely diminished and they once again because subservient to their husband. So, this request from the late Earl may have been sensible advice for Anne Devereux to keep control of her lands for her and her children.

After the death of his father in 1469, William inherited the Earldom of Pembroke, and Mary became Countess of Pembroke. Records do not show how long he studied at Lincoln's Inn but he may at this point have cut short his studies to return to Raglan to be with his wife and run the estates. During the short re-instatement of Henry VI to the throne in 1470/71 William and Mary may have undergone a worrying time as the Herbert estates, including Raglan, and the Earldom of Pembrokeshire were restored to Jasper Tudor.[10] Mary's sister, Elizabeth, was in sanctuary and Edward IV had fled across the channel and the young couple must have been fearful for their future. However, like all Yorkists, they no doubt sat tight and Edward's triumphant return in 1471 re-instated their lands and titles.

Taking over from his hugely popular father was a huge task for William and it seems he never managed to achieve the same success. He may have been more of an academic than his father, not inheriting his father's warrior character, although William did accompany Edward to France in 1475 as captain of his army.[11] Also, that same year, William was forced to exchange the earldom of Pembroke for the earldom of Huntingdon instead, with the title being awarded to Edward Prince of Wales, Mary's oldest royal nephew. Mary's nephew, Thomas Grey, Elizabeth's son from her first marriage, gave up the earldom of Huntingdon and became Marquis of Dorset at the same time.

With some resemblance of peace restored, it was in 1476 that Mary gave birth to a daughter, Elizabeth. By this time the couple has presumably established their household at Raglan. Reportedly Anne Devereux, William's mother, often resided at Chepstow Castle, another of the Herbert properties, so with William's siblings marrying and leaving home, Mary and William may have had a few years together at the beautiful Raglan as a family. Elizabeth was to be the couple's only child (or at least only surviving child) and sadly, Mary did not get to spend many years with her as she herself died in 1481 when her daughter was only five-years-old.

After Mary's death, William's royal connection was fractured and he reportedly was never as close to Edward IV as his father had been, although as the Earl of Huntingdon he was present at Edward's funeral in 1482.[12] Under Richard III's rule he experienced a slight upsurge in status and was present at Richard and Anne's coronation where he bore the queen's sceptre. He was also commissioned by Richard to raise troops to suppress the Duke of Buckingham's revolt. The Duke of Buckingham was his brother-in-law, having married Mary's younger sister Katherine, so he may have had mixed feelings about this request.

In May 1484, William married Katherine Plantagenet, the illegitimate daughter of Richard III.[13] This was likely a shrewd move by Richard to secure the Earl of Huntingdon's support in Wales. This did not quite go according to plan however and although the Herbert family gave Richard the support as due to their king in his early years, they stood back and did nothing to prevent Henry Tudor's passage through Wales after he landed on the West Coast in 1485. This infuriated Richard who had expected loyalty, but it seems the childhood bonds that were made in those early years at Raglan remained steadfast and the Herberts allowed Henry safe passage through Wales to the fields of Bosworth. William and Katherine's marriage was not a long one, with Katherine dying before 1487.

William himself died on 16th July 1490, nine years after Mary. On his death, Raglan passed into the hands of his younger brother, Walter, before ownership was eventually passed to William and Mary's daughter, Elizabeth Herbert and her husband on Sir Walter's death. An inventory of goods taken a few years after Sir Walter's demise included tapestries, bed coverings, carpets, chairs, towels silver plate, brass and pewter.[14] Many of these items would likely have been in Mary's possession during her time at the castle.

Mary's daughter, Elizabeth, Lady Herbert, had lost both her parents by the time she was fourteen and was made a ward of court. She was in attendance along with some of her other cousins at her aunt's funeral in 1492, when the dowager Queen Elizabeth was buried in a simple funeral at Windsor.[15] That same year she was married to Charles Somerset, a bastard son of Henry Beaufort, the 3rd Duke of Somerset, a marriage no doubt arranged by the king. Their daughter, Elizabeth Somerset would go on to marry William Brereton in the sixteenth century, one of the four gentleman courtiers arrested and executed as purported lovers of Anne Boleyn.

On her death, Mary relocated from one striking piece of Welsh architecture to another and like her former home of Raglan, the remains of her final resting place are today worth a visit. Both she and William are buried at Tintern Abbey, along with her mother and father-in-law, although both tombs are no longer visible today, having been destroyed along with the monastery in the 16th century. Her final journey may even have been made by boat along the nearby River Wye. William Herbert, the elder, served as the abbey's steward in the 1450s and he left provision in his will for the building of his tomb, with any surplus to be used towards the building of new cloisters.[16] The Cistercian abbey, one of the best-known monastic sites in the whole of the British Isles, was founded in the twelfth century and the Earls of Pembroke had been patrons since 1189. Although no trace remains of the two grand tombs housing William and Anne and William and Mary, they were illustrated for posterity in the Herbert Family Chronicle, the *Herbertorum Prosapia*.

Mary, along with her elder sister, Jacquetta, have the sad accolade of being the first two Woodville sisters to die, both only reaching their early thirties at most. At the time of their death, Edward and Elizabeth's reign was prospering and there was no reason to believe that wouldn't be the case for a good few years to come. For them there was no usurpation of the throne, no disappearance of their nephews, the young princes, in the tower and they would never have known of the existence of a Tudor age. Would Mary have ever dreamed that the young boy who was raised at Raglan in her household would ever go on to be the first Tudor King of England? When Mary was laid to rest in the beautiful abbey at Tintern, there would have been no concept that around fifty years later her sister's grandson, Henry VIII, would break with Rome, declare himself Head of the Church of England, and begin the greatest destruction of monastic properties that England would ever see. But then perhaps Mary's perspective of an England at peace and her sister as queen of our green and pleasant land was not such a bad ending.

Chapter Four

Margaret Woodville, Lady Maltravers

My lady Maltravers did bear a rich crysom pinned over her left breast

Margaret Woodville was the Woodville family's fifth daughter, born sometime around the year 1454. She is listed after her brother Lionel, who by all accounts was twenty-five years old when he became Dean of Exeter in 1478, placing his birth year as 1453. It is highly likely that she was named in honour of her mother's dear friend at the time, Queen Margaret of Anjou. Queen Margaret had herself given birth at the end of 1453, so the two women may have been pregnant at the same time. Just before she gave birth to her son, Prince Edward, King Henry VI had mysteriously fallen into a stupor. The royal physicians were at a loss to diagnose his condition, which came on suddenly and rendered him into a coma-like state – awake but completely unresponsive. As such, he was unable to communicate, let alone effectively rule. January 1454 saw Queen Margaret making a case for her to rule in his place until such time that her husband was recovered. She needed to safeguard herself and her newborn son, whom the king had, as yet, not even been able to acknowledge as his own. But England was not yet ready for a female ruler and her case was rejected, the council instead electing to make the Duke of York (Edward IV's father) Protector of the Realm until such time as Henry VI was well again. Jacquetta had first-hand evidence of Margaret's strength of character at this time and may have named her newest born daughter after her, as an inspirational female role-model.

Margaret, being one of the younger Woodville sisters, would have been born into a busy, vibrant household, with five surviving older brothers and four older sisters. By the time of

Margaret's entrance into the world, her eldest sister, Elizabeth, was either about to or had just married her first husband, Sir John Grey of Groby. Their first son, Thomas Grey, was also born in the early 1450s, consequently Margaret would have been of a similar age to her nephew. In 1454 Elizabeth would therefore not have been living at Grafton. The second oldest Woodville sister, Jacquetta, was also already married by the time of Margaret's birth, although still at a tender age of eight in 1454, she may or may not still have been in residence at the family home.

At the age of six, Margaret would have welcomed her oldest sister back to the family home in the saddest of circumstances after the death of her husband Sir John Grey in the second Battle of St Albans, where he had been fighting for the Lancastrian cause. For the young Margaret Woodville, despite the circumstances, it must have been exciting to have her young nephews, Thomas and his younger brother Richard, come and live at Grafton. Life would have then continued pretty much as normal until that momentous time in 1464 when Elizabeth would have broken the news to the rest of her family that she had married in secret and that she was now Queen of England. To the now ten-year-old Margaret, this must have been the stuff of dreams! Her sister was queen – therefore what possibilities would the future hold for her?

As events transpired, Margaret was the first of her unmarried sisters to be wedded in the round of marriages that followed Elizabeth's rise in status. Shortly after Edward announced to his peers at the Council of Reading that he had been secretly married for four months, arrangements began for the betrothal of Margaret to Thomas Fitzalan, Lord Maltravers, son and heir of William Fitzalan, Earl of Arundel. They were married by February 1465 when a gentleman named John Wykes sent a letter to John Paston, written *'at London, the Monday next after Saint Valentine'* (17th February 1465) which details: *Item, the Earl of Arundel's son hath wedded the queen's sister*. John Wykes was appointed in the household of Edward IV.

Thomas's parents were William Fitzalan, the 16th Earl of Arundel and 7th Baron Maltravers, and his wife, Lady Joan Neville. Joan was the eldest daughter of Richard Neville, 5th Earl of Salisbury, and therefore sister to the Earl of Warwick and a cousin to Edward IV.

The ten-year-old bride may or may not have remained at the family home until she was considered old enough to live with her husband, who was approximately four years her senior. Perhaps with all the festivities leading up to Elizabeth's coronation, Margaret remained with her family for a short time, but it is likely that at some point in 1465 she would have said goodbye to her family home at Grafton for the last time to begin her long journey to her new home and new life in West Sussex.

As Thomas was around the age of fourteen at the time of their betrothal, it may only have been a couple of years before they were considered mature enough to live as man and wife. Margaret's new home was Arundel Castle, residence of the Earls of Arundel since the 1340s, and a much grander building than her family manor at Grafton. The magnificent Arundel Castle is set high on a hill in West Sussex and Margaret must have viewed the imposing structure and her new home from a distance, long before she approached its gatehouse and entered across the drawbridge.

The Earls of Arundel had lived at the castle since at least the 1340s and the castle remained inhabited through much of the 14th and 15th centuries.[1] Five hundred years later the castle still commands the landscape with magnificent views across the South Downs and the River Arun, although only the Norman keep, medieval gatehouse and barbican would be recognisable to Margaret today.

Life at Arundel would not have been so dramatically different from her childhood to begin with. Her mother-in-Law, Joan Neville, Countess of Arundel, had died in 1462 or thereabouts so Margaret would have been in the care of her father-in-law, William. Her new husband, Thomas was the eldest of five children and the young Margaret would no doubt have joined in with their daily life, perhaps spending a large proportion of her time with Thomas' sister Mary, passing the time with needlework, perhaps music and almost certainly learning how to run a successful household. Mary's date of birth is unknown but if they were of a similar age, Margaret may have even formed a close bond with Mary that could have lasted into adulthood. Earl William was described as 'learned in an age when learning was too generally neglected' and 'a patron and friend of literature'[2] and so may have encouraged his children to be learned also – Margaret may also have had the opportunity to benefit from his example, although she already came from a family that had a love of literature, with both her mother and brother having an appreciation of the written word. Anthony Woodville would later become a patron of Caxton, who set up his first print shop in Westminster in 1476. Queen Elizabeth was also a patron, along with Anthony and William Maltravers.

As well as the castle itself, Margaret would also have known and spent time at Downley Park, the family's favourite hunting lodge, located in the vast park surrounding Arundel at Singleton. This may also have been where the wedding took place, although other sources point to the ceremony being held at Reading Abbey.

An archaeological dig was undertaken in 2014 for the lost hunting lodge of the Earls of Arundel and the results showed evidence of a high-status Tudor building on the site. The house was probably largely brick, built on stone sills. At least three types of flooring were recovered – glazed floor tiles, plain floor tiles and stone flags. Surviving correspondence between the 10th and 11th Earls of Arundel writing to Cromwell, Wolsey and King Henry VIII, also indicate that a substantial lodge building must have existed at Singleton.[3] In a much earlier description of the area, the castle and borough extent are mentioned to have two windmills called 'Tollelone' and 'Piperinge', a watermill called 'Swannebourne', a fishery with a weir, several parks and six woods with deer in the free chase of Arundel.[4] This must truly have been a beautiful place to live.

Thomas Fitzalan, styled as Lord Maltravers during the lifetime of his father, was a confirmed Yorkist, and his allegiance earned him the honour of being created a Knight of the Bath in 1461 at Edward's coronation. During Edward's reign, he remained in high favour, and was rewarded for his loyalty by being elected to the Order of the Garter in February 1474. The Order of the Garter, created by Edward III and inspired by the Legends of King Arthur, originally consisted of 24 Knights and was reserved as the highest award for loyalty and military prowess. Then in 1482, Thomas was commissioned by the king to preside over the annual feast of St George at Windsor. He was also summoned to parliament as a Baron by the title 'Thomas Arundel de Maltravers, Knight'.

Margaret would likely have accompanied her husband to many of the ceremonial events of the court, beginning with her sister's coronation and then over the years, the christening of her children. A first-hand description remains of the couple attending the baptism of Elizabeth's youngest daughter, Bridget, in 1480 at the chapel of Eltham, and was published in 'The Gentleman's Magazine' in 1831.

In the twentieth year of the reign of King Edward IV on St. Martin's Eve was born the Lady Bridget, and christened on the morning of St. Martin's Day in the Chapel of Eltham, by the Bishop of Chichester in order as ensueth:

> *First a hundred torches borne by knights, esquires, and other honest persons.*
>
> *The Lord Maltravers, bearing the basin, having a towel about his neck.*

The Earl of Northumberland bearing a taper not lit.
The Earl of Lincoln the salt.
The canopy borne by three knights and a baron.
My lady Maltravers did bear a rich crysom pinned over her left
breast.
The Countess of Richmond did bear the princess.
My lord Marquess Dorset assisted her.
My lady the king's mother, and my lady Elizabeth, were godmothers
at the font.[5]

Margaret was also given the honour of being godmother to the young princess.

And when the said princess was christened, a squire held the basins to the gossips [the godmothers], and even by the font my Lady Maltravers was godmother to the confirmation.

Thomas and Margaret also had four children of their own, although their birth dates went unrecorded: William Fitzalan; Lady Margaret Fitzalan, Countess of Lincoln; Lady Joan Fitzalan, Lady Abergavenny; and Edward Fitzalan. Their eldest son, William, was noted by Tierney to be in his forty-first year in 1524[6] which gives him an approximate birth date of 1483. This would seem unlikely as the couple would have been married for nearly nineteen years at this point and even allowing for miscarriages or children that died young and went unrecorded, it is still too big a gap. 1466 is often elsewhere given as a likely birth date for William, although Margaret would only have been twelve years old in 1466. This is still within the realms of possibility, but it is perhaps more likely that he would have been born in the early 1470s. Maybe William was in his *fifty*-first year in 1524, giving him a birth date of around 1473, which would seem more reasonable. Margaret would have been nineteen.

In 1483, the sudden death of Edward IV sent shockwaves

around the country and this and the events that followed may have caused tensions between Margaret and her husband. Immediately after Edward's death, each family had a momentous decision to make. Their loyalty to Edward IV should naturally have passed to his eldest son, Edward V, but the unexpected usurpation by Richard III and the disappearance of the two Princes, Edward and Richard, left each family having to very quickly decide whose side they were on. Whatever their personal feelings, the Earls of Arundel remained loyal to the Crown and the crown was now in the hands of Edwards's brother, Richard Duke of Gloucester. As Lord Maltravers, Thomas was present at the coronation of Richard III on 6th July 1483 and his father was also present as Earl of Arundel, accompanying Richard in the procession and performing his hereditary office of Chief Butler at the banquet that followed.[7] Did Margaret attend and was she torn between loyalty to her sister, who at the time was seeking sanctuary in Westminster Abbey, and her own loyalty to her husband and the crown? Perhaps the situation caused arguments between husband and wife. No documentary evidences places Margaret alongside her husband at the coronation, although that does not mean she was not there. Did she refuse to attend the coronation in support of her sister, or maybe she was pragmatic and realised that to keep her own family safe, she had to show respect to the new King Richard? Like so many women of this period, who found themselves with family members and loved ones on opposite sides of the divide, this must have been an anxious and perplexing time.

Thomas successfully managed to transfer his allegiance from one monarch to another (and indeed one brother to another) although it is highly possible that he already knew Richard from his time as Duke of Gloucester and therefore this may not have been a difficult transition. In 1485 Thomas was again appointed by the king to preside at the annual chapter of the garter on St George's day.

That same year, Thomas fought on Richard III's side at the Battle of Bosworth. The women of the Wars of the Roses would certainly have been more used to their husbands marching off to battle than modern women would be, but even for those battle-hardened wives, it must still have been a highly worrying time, waiting anxiously to see if their husband and loved ones would return. Thankfully Thomas did return, albeit on the losing side, but his ability to ally himself with whomever held the crown proved strong as he was subsequently pardoned by Henry VII. Perhaps Margaret intervened here, calling in a favour from her sister's eldest daughter, Elizabeth of York, the soon to be first Tudor queen. Of course, Thomas may also have earned his pardon on his own merit. How much contact Margaret would have had with her family at this time is impossible to know – did the Woodville women keep in constant correspondence or retire to their own estates to await the outcome? Her sister Elizabeth would, for the first time, have certainly been hoping for a Lancastrian victory as her plans for the union of her eldest Elizabeth, to the only son of the Lancastrian Margaret Beaufort, relied on Richard being defeated. During her time in sanctuary, the two women had plotted through Lady Margaret's physician, who acted as go-between, to join the houses of York and Lancaster once and for all. Their plan had been thwarted in 1483 when Henry Tudor had attempted to return to England but had been forced to turn back, but the idea had only been delayed. Margaret may or may not have been aware of their scheming – how much contact she would have had with her sister who after leaving sanctuary had been kept under house arrest is impossible to know.

Henry Tudor was indeed victorious, and at his coronation in October 1485, Thomas officiated as his father's deputy as chief butler. He attended the marriage of the king in January 1486 and in September of the same year, was called upon to be godfather at the coronation of Prince Arthur. Then on 25th November 1487,

Thomas bore the Rod and Dove at the coronation of Elizabeth of York. Margaret may have accompanied him to at least the last two of these events, happy to see her niece take up the position of Queen of England. Details of these ceremonial events are given by Leland, and although Margaret is not named officially, she would most likely have been a part of the number of 'dyvers other gentlewomen'.

In 1487 William, Earl of Arundel died, and Thomas succeeded to the earldom, becoming the 17th Earl of Arundel and making Margaret the Countess of Arundel. How far she had come from the ten-year-old girl playing with her siblings at Grafton.

In November 1489 a four-year-old Prince Arthur was escorted by Thomas, Earl of Arundel and the Marquis of Berkeley into the presence of his father, King Henry, to receive the order of Knighthood. Margaret and Thomas' eldest son, William Maltravers, along with eighteen others, was made a Knight of the Bath. That same year, Thomas was made Warden of the New Forest, obtaining with his office a fee to himself and his heirs of 40 shillings a year from the Abbey of Reading along with numerous other benefits.[8] Thomas and his family were still riding high in the esteem of their monarchs.

The exact date of Margaret's death is unknown, but it is believed to be around 1490, aged around thirty-five. Whether Margaret and Thomas had a happy marriage or not can only be guessed at. It is enticing, however, to imagine that the fact that Thomas never remarried, even though he outlived her by thirty-four years, illustrates the love they had for each other in his choice to not take another wife. Charles Carracioli writing in the eighteenth century described Thomas as 'preferring country life to the trappings of the court' and credits him with being a gracious and indulgent master, a tender and affectionate husband, and an excellent father. 'His gentleness, modesty and piety made him beloved and respected by all parties'. If he was indeed all these things, then perhaps Margaret did lead a happy life with him. Margaret was buried in the Collegiate Chapel at Arundel.

After her death, Thomas remained in Henry's favour, retiring from court during his advanced years to the seclusion of his house at Downley. He died at Downley Park on 25th October 1524, at a grand old age, well into his seventies. There are two memorials in Singleton church to Thomas and his son William, who also died at the lodge in 1544, either side of the altar. William was named as his executor and Thomas left instruction in his will that he wished to be 'buryd in the chancel of my colledg church of Arundell, where my ladye my wife doth lie'.[9]

Their eldest son, William, succeeded to the earldom and led a mostly quiet life. One event of note was his being called to sit as one of the peers at the trial of Anne Boleyn and her brother George, Lord Rochford. His eldest son, Henry, also sat on the jury at Anne's trial as Henry, Lord Maltravers. On William's death in 1544, Henry (Margaret's grandson) succeeded his father, becoming the 19th Earl. He led a much more tumultuous life than either his father or grandfather. A staunch catholic, he was active in helping Mary I succeed to the throne. During her sister Elizabeth's reign, he became involved in the plot to overthrow the queen and replace her with Mary Queen of Scots and found himself thrown into prison, although he was later released. On his death, having no surviving sons, the title of Earl of Arundel passed into the Howard family line of the dukes of Norfolk through the marriage of his daughter Mary. His other daughter married Lord Lumley, who in honour of his wife's family created the memorial stone that can be seen today in the Fitzalan Chapel of Arundel Castle.

Margaret is safely ensconced in the chapel in the grounds of her family home, and her tomb can be visited today. At the castle, the Fitzalan family line is now viewed as a separate creation of the earldom, and consequently if you visit the Fitzalan chapel at the castle, the 17th Earl (Thomas) is known as the 10th Earl, with his son and grandson being known as the 11th, and 12th Earls of Arundel.[10] The remains of the earls, along with Margaret's are within the vaults beneath the Fitzalan Chapel. The inscription on the brass plaque was noted by Mark Tierney in his *History and Antiquities of the Castle and Town of Arundel*:

In this tomb doth rest the bodies of the Right Hon. Thomas, Earl of Arundel, Baron Maltravers, and of Clyme, &c. Knight of the Most Noble order of the Garter, who married Lady Margaret, one of the heiresses of Richard Woodvile, Earl of Rivers, sister to Elizabeth, Queen of England, some time wife to King Edward IV: which Thomas Died anno fifteen of King Henry VIII. 1524; And William, also Earl of Arundel, his son, Baron Maltravers, and of Clyme, &c. Knight of the said most Noble Order of the Garter, who married Anne, daughter of Henry Percy, Earl of Northumberland; which William died, anno thirty-five of Henry VIII, and was father to Henry, the last Earl of Arundel, entombed in this church at Arundel, where is placed for remembrance,

Johem, Barone Lumley, 1596.[11]

Chapter Five

Jane Woodville, Lady Grey of Ruthin

Come what come may, time and the hour runs through the roughest day

Jane is unquestionably one of the more mysterious of the Woodville sisters, with even her Christian name varying from source to source. Sometimes referred to as Joan, and oddly other times as Eleanor, she was the second youngest Woodville girl to be born, sometime around 1455 to 1456.

Jane's chosen husband was Anthony Grey, eldest son of Edmund, Lord Grey of Ruthin and the couple were married in or around February 1466 when Jane would have been about eleven years old. Anthony's birth date is not recorded, but his younger brother, George Grey was said to have been born c.1455.[1] For Jane and Anthony to be considered a good match, they would likely have been of a similar age, so it is safe to assume that Anthony was probably born in the early 1450s.

Anthony's father, Edmund Grey, had been born at Ruthin Castle around 1420 and became the 4th Lord Grey de Ruthin in 1440, succeeding to the title on the death of his grandfather. Initially a Lancastrian, Edmund notably switched sides during the Battle of Northampton in 1460. In an account of the battle, Edmund Grey and his men were positioned on the right flank of the battlefield on the Lancastrian side, but for some reason early on in the fighting, Grey decided to defect, and join the Yorkists. This threw the Lancastrian side into confusion and is considered to have contributed hugely to the Lancastrian defeat.[2] After the fray, Henry VI was captured and taken into custody by the Earl of Warwick, although it wasn't until the following year, after the bloody battle on the snow-covered fields of Towton that the

Yorkists finally took the throne. As a reward for his loyalty, and in honour of his new queen's coronation, Edward bestowed upon Edmund the earldom of Kent on 30th May 1465. His eldest son, and Jane's future husband, Anthony Grey was also knighted in the Tower on the eve of Elizabeth's coronation.[3]

Although the De Grey family seat had been Ruthin Castle, when Edmund became Earl of Kent, he no longer used the castle as a residence, allowing it to become uninhabited and neglected, preferring his properties closer to court.[4] The De Grey family also held numerous properties in Bedfordshire, particularly the manor of Silsoe which had been in the family since 1284. The first member of the De Grey family that can be firmly linked to Bedfordshire is John de Grey of Shirland (about 1205-1266). Although he inherited Shirland in Derbyshire, he acquired most of his wealth through royal service and marriage. As Edmund and his family became more involved with the Yorkist court, Bedfordshire would have been a more convenient base for travelling to London and the court.

Once married in early 1466, the young couple would have no doubt journeyed to one of the family's Bedfordshire manors to live together under the care of Edmund and his wife, Katherine Countess of Kent, daughter of Henry Percy, the 2nd Earl of Northumberland. Here, Jane would have been taken under Katherine's wing and tutored in all she needed to know to become a successful wife and mother and to manage a household. Although for females, leaving home after marriage to live with in-laws was customary, this must still have been a daunting prospect for a young woman who was not yet twelve years old. Jane can only have hoped for as kind a mother-in-law as the future Elizabeth of York aimed to be. Writing to her prospective daughter-in-law's parents, Ferdinand and Isabella in 1498, Elizabeth desired to hear news of Katherine's health, whom she described as our common daughter: 'we wish and desire from our heart that we may often and speedily hear of the health and safety of your serenity, and of the health and safety of the aforesaid most illustrious Lady Katherine, who we think of and esteem as our own daughter...'.[5] For Jane, the Countess of Kent would from 1466 onwards have become her substitute mother in her own mother's absence.

In the fourteenth to sixteenth centuries, lordship was often peripatetic with the household travelling between properties remaining for a few weeks or months, before moving to another of their residences. The day to day running of each of their estates was left in the hands of a steward in their absence. Edmund's chief residence after 1465 was Wrest Park, so it is highly likely that Anthony and Jane would have lived here, perhaps visiting and staying at other properties in the locality as the need arose. Wrest Park nowadays is a splendid Georgian mansion, set in beautifully designed gardens, yet the house would be completely unrecognisable to Jane today, with the medieval mansion having been demolished in the 1830s when the current house was built. Landscape investigations into the medieval manor at Wrest Park evidence that an old manor house had been in existence there since at least the 1200s, with the first park being documented there in 1344.[6] In a lease of the house in 1512, Wrest Park was recorded as 'the mansion house with the moat', fishponds and an orchard. Investigations show there would have been a great hall, as was typical of castles and manor houses of the period, with a domestic block across the eastern end. John, the 2nd Lord Grey of Wilton, added a chapel to the house in 1320.

Edmund Grey, Anthony's father, continued to extend the family's Bedfordshire estates in the late 1400s, the most notable purchase being Ampthill Castle in 1473 which he purchased on the death of its previous owner. Sir John Cornwall, Lord Fanhope. Ampthill quickly became a second favoured residence of the family alongside Wrest Park. By 1473 Anthony and Jane would have been around eighteen years of age, so perhaps by acquiring Ampthill, they were able to leave Wrest Park and set up their own home together? Or with Anthony away at court with his father, maybe Jane remained living with her mother-in-law and his younger siblings, moving between the two residences as required?

Ampthill Castle is today marked only by Katherine's Cross on the approximate site of the palace. The cross is named after its most famous future resident, Katherine of Aragon who lived there during her divorce proceedings from Henry VIII in 1533. The castle was built in the early 1400s when Sir John married Elizabeth, sister of Henry IV, and wanted a suitably 'royal' residence for his royal spouse. It consisted of four wings, forming a rectangle around an inner court. The north wing contained the obligatory Great Hall and the east wing held the kitchens and gatehouse. The castle also boasted state rooms and private apartments for the family. Outside the north wing was a smaller court which contained a well-house. By 1555 the buildings had fallen into a state of disrepair and the castle was demolished at some point before 1649.

Whether it was at Wrest or Ampthill, Jane's day to day life would have been taken up with running the household and the estate, spending her leisure time no doubt taking walks in the beautiful grounds surrounding her homes. Particularly amongst the nobility, managing even a modest household could be a huge undertaking with upwards of twenty to thirty staff to oversee. Her husband, Anthony, may often have been away on court business, although with a father still living and very much active, many of his court duties may have been ceremonial. Edward IV, by all accounts, did hold Anthony in high esteem and considered him a kinsman and he was one of the lords present at Westminster on 3rd July 1471 to witness Edward Prince of Wales invested as heir to the throne. He also journeyed to France with the king, where in August 1475 he was present to witness the treaty between Edward IV and King Louis XI, agreeing to a seven-year truce and free trade between the two countries.

Anthony was also present at the ten-day festivities held in July 1476 for the re-interment of Edward's father, the Duke of York and his younger brother, Edmund Earl of Rutland, both of whom were killed in 1460. The cortege taking his father and brother from Pontefract Priory where they had been hastily buried after the Battle of Wakefield began at the priory, with Richard Duke of Gloucester as the chief mourner. The procession met up with Edward and the court at Northampton and in a rare sign of unity all three York brothers escorted their father and brother to the family mausoleum at Fotheringhay. Queen Elizabeth was present, along with her brother Anthony, her two daughters and eldest son Thomas, and Anthony Grey was also with the Royal procession.[7] As Michael Hicks points out, the heralds may simply have ignored the Ladies as many are not listed, but it is very possible that Jane was also with her sister and husband on this occasion.

Outside of court life, both Anthony and his parents were staunch Roman Catholics and in 1475 he and Jane were listed as brethren of the confraternity of the Holy Trinity at Luton, along with Edmund and Katherine Grey.[8] Religious guilds such as this were set up by a group of individuals in a locality, with a common faith and vision and members of the group would often meet and dine together. The Luton Holy Trinity guild was composed of the most illustrious men connected with Luton and was founded by Thomas Rotherham, Lord Chancellor in 1474, with the first register commencing in 1475.[9]

Sadly, Anthony did not live a long life, dying in November 1480, when he was probably in his late twenties. His premature death is certainly part of the reason why we are unable today to trace much detail of their life together. Edmund Grey would outlive his son by another ten years, and as Anthony never inherited the earldom of Kent, in many records he is just afforded a brief mention. It is his younger brother George, who became the second Earl of Kent in 1490, who appears more frequently in accounts. George Grey, of course, married Jane's sister Anne in or around 1483. However, in death Anthony received more recognition than in life perhaps. Buried in the abbey church of St Albans, he is commemorated by a wonderful brass plaque, allegedly paid for by Elizabeth Woodville. The brass is in front of the High Altar where he was buried and displays him with tattered mantling, resting on his tilting helmet, illustrating that he had taken part in many battles. He also wears a Yorkist collar of suns and roses, a connection to the 'Sunne in Splendour' emblem adopted by Edward IV.[10]

Jane was only twenty-five years old when her husband died – their life together had hardly begun. It is thought that the couple remained childless during their ten-year marriage which could signify that theirs was a loveless marriage, or perhaps there was a medical reason why they could not conceive, although they may of course have experienced unrecorded still births or children that didn't survive beyond their early years. However, a reference to an unknown Lady Katherine Grey in the records could refute that. In 1482, the Yorkist princess Mary died, and Jane Woodville attended her funeral, her position in the account implies she may even have been chief mourner. Mary died on either the Monday or the Thursday before Whit Sunday (accounts differ) and was buried at Windsor a week later. On Monday 28th May, her body was bought to lay in Greenwich parish church surrounded by four tapers, beginning the first stage of her journey to her final resting place. The Ladies were headed by 'my Lady Grey of Ruthinne, the quenes sister, my Lady Strange (probably Joan, daughter of Jacquetta and John Lestrange), my Lady Dame Katherine Grey, my Lady (daughter/dacre), Lady Mastresse, Mistress Cowyll Lyle, Mistress Gyfforde and other gentlewomen'.[11] This list of mourners mentions a Lady Katherine Grey and there is a suggestion that Katherine Grey may have been the daughter of Jane and Anthony. There are two primary sources that describe the funeral, one of them has 'My Lady Daughter', the other 'My Lady Dacre' in the list of mourners, after Katherine's name. As wife to Lord Dacre, the queen's chamberlain, Lady Dacre would likely have been in attendance so the word 'daughter' may be an error. Dame Katherine Grey is also listed among the mourners at the funeral of Elizabeth Woodville ten years later in 1492, which was attended by several of her sister's children. Most of Elizabeth's sisters had pre-deceased her, but several of her nieces came to her funeral, including Elizabeth Stafford (daughter of Katherine Woodville), and Elizabeth, Lady Herbert (daughter of Mary Woodville).

If she were a child of Jane and Anthony, born in the early years of their marriage, Katherine could have been as old as fifteen at Princess Mary's funeral and therefore of a similar age to the young princess. They may have been close as cousins, even playmates, indicating that Jane remained very much involved in her sister Elizabeth's life at court. The same Dame Katherine is also recorded at Prince Arthur's christening in 1486 and the Coronation of Elizabeth of York in 1487. At all these occasions, she is listed as Dame Katherine Grey so it seems she remained an unmarried woman, perhaps never having had a marriage arranged for her after the death of her father and possibly living at court in service. Other than her Grey surname, there is no firm evidence that she was Jane and Anthony's daughter, but it is a possibility and the idea cannot be discounted.

After 1480, Jane's life story becomes somewhat entwined with that of her sister, Anne, leading to some confusion. In 1482, the widowed Jane is still being styled as Lady Grey de Ruthin at Princess Mary's funeral. However sometime around 1483, Anne Woodville married George Grey, who after Anthony's death also became Lord Grey of Ruthin, suggesting Anne would also have been known by the title 'Lady Grey'. A 'Lady Grey de Ruthyn' attended Prince Arthur's christening in 1486 and is also mentioned as part of the celebrations for Elizabeth of York's coronation in 1487. These references could refer to Jane IF she remained a widow, but there is some evidence that she may have remarried, so the later references to 'Lady Grey de Ruthyn' could actually refer to her sister, Anne.

But what of this possible rumoured second marriage for Jane? Sometime, likely after 1482, it is suggested that Jane may have married Edward Wingfield, one of the Wingfield brothers of Letheringham. Edward Wingfield was an older brother of Richard Wingfield, who would go on to marry Katherine Woodville in the 1490s, and perhaps, as is later suggested with Richard and Katherine, Edward may have served as a member of Jane's household. Sons of Sir John Wingfield and Elizabeth Fitzlewis, Edward and Richard came from a large family of twelve sons and four daughters; Edward is believed to have been born about 1453. Again, between Jane and Anne uncertainty arises with some accounts stating that it was Anne who married Edward Wingfield. However, this seems highly unlikely as we know that Edward was still alive in 1486 and as Anne had married George Grey by 1483, she would have had to have married and divorced Edward to marry George.

The more likely scenario is that it was indeed Jane that married Edward, presumably sometime after 1482/3. That Edward can be linked to the Woodville family is illustrated by the fact that he accompanied Jane's brother, Edward Woodville, to Granada where they fought alongside Ferdinand and Isabella in 1486. Wingfield was knighted by Edward Woodville that same year in Granada.[12] If he wasn't a member of her household, it could even have been through her brother that an introduction was made?

After Anthony's death, Jane received the manors of Thurleigh in Bedfordshire and Wootton in Northamptonshire as her Dower and perhaps she resided at one of these locations, first as a widow and secondly with her new husband.[13] No date is given for her death and with Edward Wingfield being only a mere Knight and also only afforded the briefest of mentions, Jane seems to fall completely out of the picture.

It seems she was still living on 24th September 1485 when she was mentioned in a grant that was awarded to her brother, Edward Woodville:

Grant to Sir Edward Wydeville of 50l. per annum out of the issues of the lordships and manors of Kyrtlyngton ..... If the said Edward should die without such heirs then the said 50l. shall remain to Sir Richard Wydeville, brother of the said Edward Wydeville, and the heirs of his body issuing; and if the said Richard will die without heirs of his body begotten, then the said 50l. shall remain to Anne, Margaret, and Joan [Jane], daughters of Jaquetta, late duchess of Bedford, and Elizabeth daughter of Mary, daughter of the same Jaquetta, and the heirs of their bodies lawfully begotten; and if the said Anne, Margaret, Joan and Elizabeth shall die without such heirs, then the said 50l shall remain to Elizabeth, late queen of the aforesaid Edward, late King of England, and Katharine, duchess of Bucks, and the heirs of their bodies lawfully begotten... [14]

She had, however, died by 4th August 1492 when a post mortem inquisition was taken after the death of her brother Richard, when his only sibling mentioned amongst his heirs was their sister Katherine, Duchess of Bedfordshire. Also mentioned were various nieces and nephews including Anne Woodville's son, Henry, Earl of Essex, Margaret Woodville's son William, Lord Maltravers, Mary Woodville's daughter, Elizabeth, Lady Herbert and Jacquetta Woodville's daughter, Joan, Lady Strange. There is no mention of Katherine Grey.

The inheritance of the de Grey estates passed from George Grey, upon his death in 1505, to Sir Richard Grey, 3rd Earl of Kent, his heir from his marriage to Anne Woodville. Richard Grey, it seems, was a gambler and found himself heavily in debt. He wasted most of his estate, selling the manor and castle of Ruthin and Ampthill to the Crown, and mortgaging Wrest Park to Sir Henry Wyatt, although Wrest was successfully bought back years later by his half-brother, Henry, 4th Earl of Kent.

In her death as in her life, Jane remains an enigma with her final resting place unknown. What we do know of her life throws out more questions than answers: did she have a child, did she remarry, how did she feel about her sister Anne residing at Ampthill and Wrest Park after her second marriage, where Jane herself had once planned a future with her husband Anthony? But lack of evidence about her life does not mean she lived an uninteresting life. Although sad, widowhood was often expected, and widows often had much more freedom than their married counterparts. Jane was probably not considered wealthy enough or dynastically important enough for the crown to arrange a second marriage for her, so her circumstances may have afforded her the freedom to live peacefully on her dower lands and perhaps find a second husband of her choosing. Her life may not have been as eventful as some of the other Woodville women, but maybe her sister's choice in 1464 to marry the King of England earned Jane a life that she would consider well-lived.

Chapter Six

Katherine Woodville, Duchess of Buckingham

the Duchesses having on ther Heds Coronatts of Golde richely garnyshed with Perle and precious stones

From high up on the shoulders of a squire, the six-year-old Katherine looked around her in wonder as her elder sister, Elizabeth, slipped off her shoes. The imposing structure of Westminster Abbey loomed up in front of them – the location of every coronation since the time of William the Conqueror, and today was to be Elizabeth's turn. Her sister looked beautiful, 'clothed in a mantyll of purpull & a coronall upon hir hede'.[1] Surrounding Katherine, and following in the footsteps of her sister, were ladies, in dresses of red or scarlet and knights dressed in blue gowns with white hoods. As the procession continued, Katherine herself approached the door to the abbey, alongside her husband Henry Stafford, Duke of Buckingham, known to all as Harry. From their viewpoint, with Harry also perched high up on a squire's shoulders, the pair had the best view of proceedings. Her sister was about to be crowned Queen of England, and she Katherine, was a duchess. Her family were very important indeed!

Katherine Woodville was the youngest of Elizabeth's sisters, born around 1458. Her own wedding, to the ten-year-old Duke of Buckingham, had taken place early in 1465, as she was titled the Duchess of Buckingham at Elizabeth's coronation. Her husband, Henry Stafford, born in September 1454, was the eldest of the two Stafford brothers, and he and his younger brother Humphrey had both been knighted in honour of Elizabeth's coronation. Their father, also called Humphrey, had died in

1458, never achieving the title Duke of Buckingham having died during his own father's lifetime. Harry's grandfather, also called Humphrey, followed two years later in July 1460, when he was killed fighting on the side of the Lancastrians in the Battle of Northampton, allegedly whilst guarding Henry VI's tent. As the oldest grandson, Harry, at the tender age of four, inherited the dukedom. As a minor, his estates passed into the custody of his grandmother Anne Stafford, the Duchess of Buckingham. Anne was an older sister of Cecily, Duchess of York and therefore Edward IV's aunt.

The young Henry and Humphrey Stafford were a concern to the Yorkist regime as they were descended from Edward III, and therefore had a tenuous claim to the throne themselves. Their paternal grandmother, Anne Stafford was born a Neville. Her father, Ralph Neville, had married Joan Beaufort, daughter of John of Gaunt and his mistress (later wife) Katherine Swynford. Their grandfather, Humphrey Stafford, was the son of Anne of Gloucester, daughter of Thomas of Woodstock. Both Thomas and John of Gaunt were sons of Edward III. No doubt because of their 'proximity' to the throne, Edward IV purchased their wardships from the Dowager Duchess in February 1464, and for a while Harry, at least, was in the custody of Edward's older sister, Anne, Duchess of Exeter.

When she became Queen, Elizabeth Woodville was given guardianship of the young Buckinghams and both they and Katherine were bought up together at court, with Elizabeth receiving 500 marks yearly for their maintenance.[2] Having resided at court from such an early age, Katherine out of all the Woodville sisters, may have had few memories of her early years at Grafton. With the resilience of youth, she no doubt would have settled quickly into her new life. With her own mother Jacquetta also spending much of her life now at court, she would have likely still been in her care, and would also have been able to spend some time with her elder sister Anne, who served as one of Elizabeth's ladies. Being raised alongside her new husband, the pair would have had a chance to get to know each other and then as the royal nursery began to fill up, Katherine would have no doubt also spent time with her royal nieces. Indeed, she appears in later life to have been close with the eldest York Princess, Elizabeth, which may be a friendship that had begun in those early years at court.

In September 1470, the seemingly secure world Katherine inhabited was thrown into turmoil when King Edward was forced to flee into exile and her sister, the queen, fled into sanctuary. Katherine would have been about twelve years old and how much she would have understood or been aware of at the time about the danger to her family cannot be known, but this may certainly have been her first awakening to the dangerous world she lived in. It is thought that at this time, custody of Harry and his brother was reverted to his grandmother, so perhaps the young Katherine was also sent there too. She may also have taken sanctuary with her elder sister and mother, although there is no specific mention of her, or perhaps she remained in the care of her elder sister, Anne, whose location at this time is also unknown. Either way, this would have been a huge period of uncertainty for her. For the first time, Katherine may have realised that beneath the dazzle of court life, danger was never far away.

However, eight months later, in 1471, order was restored as Edward made a triumphant return to London, and Katherine's fifteen-year-old husband accompanied him, presumably meeting up with him on his journey back to the capital. On the death of Henry VI that same year, Harry became the sole surviving heir to the de Bohun estates. Upon the death of Humphrey de Bohun in 1373, his vast estates were left to his two daughters, Eleanor de Bohun who married Thomas of Woodstock, and Mary de Bohun who married Henry Bolingbroke, who became Henry IV. The inheritance was withheld from Harry by Edward IV, presumably because the lands were worth over £1000 to the Crown at the time, but also perhaps because they emphasised Buckingham's descent from royalty. It was this inheritance that many historians believe point to Harry's dissatisfaction with the Yorkist regime. But, being a ward of the court did have its benefits, and Harry was able to come into other of his estates three years before his coming of age.[3] In 1473, at the age of seventeen, he received part of one the richest inheritances in England, with most of the land he received being in Wales.

We will never know how much resentment Harry bore towards Edward or towards his wife and her family. Sources claim that he despised his marriage, that he felt Katherine was beneath him and that he was unhappy with the de Bohun estates being denied to him. At court he was welcomed but often side-lined, his duties being in the most part ceremonial, although on occasions he was given responsibility such as he had in 1478 when he was made High Steward of England and had the dubious honour of sentencing the king's brother, George Duke of Clarence, to death.

At some point, likely around the time he came into some of his inheritance, the young couple would have been considered old enough to leave court and set up home as man and wife. Their destination was probably Brecon Castle in Wales as it was here in 1478 that their first child was born, a son they named Edward, in honour of their king, who stood as godfather to the child, giving a gift of a gold cup.

Brecon is situated in the March borderland, the divide between England and Wales. The castle itself was in a beautiful location, overlooking both the River Usk and the River Honddu in the heart of the town. Entrance to the castle was by one of two gates, both approached across a drawbridge, with a curtain wall enclosing the castle within. As with most castles, the grandest part of the building was the great hall, the social nucleus of the castle. Katherine and her husband would also have enjoyed private apartments, which were situated next to the hall. References to other rooms and buildings in the medieval documents include a chapel, exchequer, kitchen, harness tower, stable and porter's chamber .[4]

Leaving the hustle and bustle of the court must have bought mixed emotions for Katherine, perhaps sad to leave her family and the life she had known for the last ten years, but excited to become mistress of her own domain. Settling into married life, two more children followed in quick succession, a daughter Elizabeth was born in 1479, followed by a second son Henry who was also born around 1479/80. The couple may also have had a third son, Humphrey, who did not live for very long.

As the year 1482 ended, and 1483 dawned, Katherine once again found herself with child, and no doubt she busied herself preparing for a peaceful pregnancy and confinement. But then in April 1483, news of the king's death meant that for Katherine, the wheel of fortune span again and her life was about to take another dramatic turn.

On hearing the news of the king's death, his younger brother Richard, Duke of Gloucester, wrote to London proffering his loyalty to Edward's son and heir. He then began the long journey down from his home in the north of England to the capital. Simultaneously Edward's young son, the now Edward V, was being escorted to London by his older brother Richard Grey, and his uncle, Anthony Woodville, Earl Rivers, who had been with the young prince at Ludlow. Harry Buckingham met with Gloucester en route on 29th April and they lodged that evening in Northampton, sharing a meal with Rivers and Richard Grey who had ridden to meet them, leaving the young prince behind at Stony Stratford. By all accounts the meal was convivial, with all four men enjoying each other's company. The next day, 30th April, they all began their journey to meet up with new king at Stony Stratford, eighteen miles south of Northampton. But Rivers and Grey never reached their destination, along the route the two dukes pulled their horses up and informed the pair that they were under arrest. They then rode off to meet Edward to escort him to London, ordering Rivers and Grey be taken to one of Gloucester's northern castles as prisoners.[5]

Hearing the news, and fearing for her life and family, Elizabeth once again fled into sanctuary, with her daughters, her younger son Prince Richard, and her eldest son, Thomas Grey. They were soon joined in sanctuary by one of the Woodville brothers, Lionel. Edward arrived shortly in London, escorted by Gloucester and Buckingham, where preparations for the young king's coronation were underway. However, on their arrival, the coronation was immediately delayed. What followed then is well documented – on 27th May Gloucester was appointed Lord Protector, and on 10th and 11th June he wrote to the City of York and to Lord Neville (his mother's family) asking them to bring troops 'to aid and assist us against the Queen, her bloody adherents and affinity; which have intended and daily doth intend to murder and utterly destroy us and our cousin the Duke of Buckingham and the old royal blood of the realm'.[6] Then came the accusations in June that Edward IV's marriage to Elizabeth was invalid as he was already pre-contracted to an Eleanor Butler, and the even more salacious rumours that Edward was a bastard son, a result of his mother's affair, a hugely controversial claim considering Cecily Neville, mother to Edward and Richard, was still alive.

Harry Buckingham played a hugely active role in Richard's eventual usurpation of throne. What thoughts could possibly be going through Katherine's mind at home in Brecon as news of these events filtered through? Even if their marriage was an unhappy one, the couple had known each other since childhood and had had four, possibly five children together. Spending all these years in each other's company, they may surely have found some common ground to forge a marriage together, or at the very least a respect for each other. If so, Katherine must have been horrified at this stage to hear news of her sister's plight and her husband's involvement with it all. Each piece of news she received seemed to get progressively worse, culminating in the awful news that her brother Anthony and nephew, Richard Grey, had been executed without trial. Whatever the state of their marriage beforehand, Katherine must have been sick to the stomach with puzzlement, fear and worry.

So, it was on 6th July 1483 that Richard III, and his wife Anne Neville were jointly crowned at Westminster. Harry, recently appointed Constable of England headed the large entourage through the streets of London. Katherine was understandably not present. For Harry's part, he had finally been promised the remaining estates of the De Bohun inheritance, which he finally obtained in July 1483.[7] It does not take a huge stretch of the imagination to think that this may have played a large part in his support of Richard, perhaps also believing that under Richard, he would play a more important role at court than he ever would be able to under the part-Woodville king, Edward V.

However, something changed dramatically in the next few weeks and on 24th September, Buckingham defected, leaving Richard who was on progress to the North and returning to his home in Brecon. One wonders what sort of reception he received from Katherine! Whilst there, it is thought that he was persuaded by John Morton, Bishop of Ely, who was being held captive at the castle, to turn coat. John Morton had been an important part of Edward IV's court and was an executor of his will. When Richard III took power, he was immediately arrested and held in custody at Brecon. It is thought that John Morton put Harry in touch with Elizabeth Woodville and Margaret Beaufort, who were conspiring together to arrange the marriage of the eldest York princess to Margaret's son, Henry Tudor. No doubt Katherine also took some part in persuading her husband to aid her sister's plans. Harry then wrote to the exiled Henry Tudor asking him to bring an army to assist in overthrowing Richard. He then began to do the same himself, assembling men and arms at Brecon castle. By Saturday 18th October, he was ready to move, aiming to meet up with his nephew Thomas Grey, who had escaped sanctuary and was also raising men. But nature was to prove a valiant enemy, and in a flood of torrential rain he reached the River Severn to discover the banks had burst and had to turn back. Many of his men, who had been never been that keen to fight in the first place, defected.

Having to quickly revise his plans, he decided to make his way to Weobley, in Herefordshire, leaving his daughters, one who would have been a newborn, at home in Brecon. Katherine and his two sons accompanied him to Herefordshire, to the home of Lord Ferrers. This act in itself appears to be an indicator that Katherine and Harry did have some sort of respect for each other, with the pair working together towards a common goal. From Weobley, Buckingham continued tried to raise an army, but the men of Herefordshire wouldn't rise, hearing reports that the king and his army were on their way.

By now Buckingham was a wanted man with a reward on his head. In the meantime, his castle in Wales had been raided and seized by members of the Vaughan family, loyal to the king, who looted the castle and took his daughters into their custody. Realising they were in trouble, Katherine and Harry's oldest son was disguised as a girl and smuggled away by loyal retainers and Buckingham (presumably with Katherine) went into hiding in Shropshire in the house of his servant, Ralph Bannister. But Bannister sold him out and on 1st November he was captured and taken to Richard at Salisbury, where the following day he was beheaded in the marketplace, without trial. Katherine and her younger son were taken to London.

Whatever their marital relationship, the end of 1483 would have found Katherine at an extremely low ebb. Her husband was dead, and she was facing the likelihood of never seeing her home in Brecon again. Where she lived whilst in London is not documented, but early in 1484 Richard allowed Katherine to convey her two daughters and eldest son to London, her youngest son was already with her having been captured with her in Herefordshire. When her sister Elizabeth finally left sanctuary, she was more or less placed under house arrest and the same fate may have been meted out to Katherine.

But as it does, the wheel of fortune continued spinning and once again Katherine's fortune was soon to change. After his aborted first attempt to return to England and raise an army, Henry Tudor and his supporters finally landed in Pembrokeshire and in the autumn of 1485, Richard III was defeated on the Bosworth Battlefield. One of Henry VII's early acts was to reverse the attainder and restore Katherine's dowry. She also found herself the subject of what was most probably another arranged marriage to Jasper Tudor, the newly created Duke of Bedford. Henry's uncle, Jasper Tudor, had been by Henry's side for most of his life, sharing his years of exile. His father, Edmund Tudor, had died before Henry was born and his uncle had played a huge role in his upbringing. No contemporary source gives the date of their marriage, but by the time Jasper attended the first sitting of parliament, on 7th November 1485, he was stated to be married.[8] Katherine was 27, Jasper was 54.

Just before Henry's coronation in October 1485, Katherine's eldest son by her first husband, the seven-year-old Edward, was created a Knight of the Bath. The wardship of both her sons was awarded to the king's mother, the formidable Lady Margaret Beaufort, and the boys grew up in her household – her daughters probably remained with Katherine. In parliament the duchess was awarded 1000 marks per year from her late husband's will and extensive lands in England and Wales.

For the first Christmas of the new Tudor era, Jasper and Katherine remained at court and Katherine was given a gift of a golden goblet.[9] Compared to the Christmases of the last couple of years, Katherine was once again able to celebrate the seasonal festivities amongst family, perhaps even with a hint of optimism returning. Then on 18th January 1486, Elizabeth Woodville and Margaret Beaufort's plan finally came to fruition, and the Houses of York and Lancaster were united by the wedding of Henry and Elizabeth. Although not much detail has survived about the celebrations, there is no doubt that Katherine and Jasper, probably still in attendance at court after the Christmas celebrations, would have been there to help the couple celebrate. Up and down the country bonfires were lit, and the city of London rejoiced, celebrating the occasion with dancing and singing and looking, no doubt, to a more peaceful future.[10]

With the seasonal and wedding festivities over, it would soon have been time to leave court and for Katherine to begin married life for the second time. She was no doubt much worldlier than the teenager who had left for Brecon ten years earlier. On 22nd March 1486, Jasper was awarded a substantial amount of properties, including Minster Lovell (from the attainted Viscount Lovell, one of Richard's closest associates), and this, along with Sudeley Castle, became one of the couple's favourites residences.

Once again, Katherine who may have been living quite simply since the death of her first husband, suddenly had some glorious properties to inhabit. The magnificent Sudeley Castle in Winchcombe in Gloucestershire had previously belonged to Richard III, firstly for a short spell when he was Duke of Gloucester and again when ownership was returned to him when he became king. It was Richard who arranged for the magnificent banqueting hall to be built at the castle, with oriel windows and adjoining state rooms. Sudeley Castle is still a remarkable building to visit today, although only the shell of the banqueting hall remain. Only the ruins of Minster Lovell remain today but even they are idyllic, nestling against the banks of the River Windrush. With the buildings grouped around a central courtyard, the medieval manor boasted an entrance hall with a beautifully cloistered roof, a great hall, first floor apartments and a private chapel. The east wing consisted of the stable and kitchens. Their other favoured residence, Thornbury Castle, belonged to the Stafford family and seems to have been theirs through Katherine's dowry. On her death, it passed to her eldest son, Edward, but during their time together it reportedly became one of Jasper's favourite residences.

Towards the end of March 1486, Jasper headed off for South Wales and sent £50 to Katherine who was recorded as staying at the Abbey of Stratford near London.[11] Could this have been her residence during her widowhood, that she returned to before taking up home with her new husband? Stratford Abbey, like many others, became a victim of the dissolution in the sixteenth century but it was reportedly a favourite of Edward IV who donated two casks of wine annually for masses to be said for his soul. Maybe this choice of destination for Katherine upon leaving court could indicate she had stayed there previously, perhaps for a while during Richard's reign?

When Jasper was not on court business, the couple seem to have split their time between Thornbury Manor, Sudeley Castle and Minster Lovell. Jasper's household was seemingly dominated by many of his wife's former servants[12] with the most senior position of chamberlain being filled by Sir Edward Montfort, once a steward in the Duke of Buckingham's household. Having been in exile, Jasper would not have had household servants, so it seems he was happy to allow his wife to fill these positions, which she did choosing loyal staff from her time in Brecon. Perhaps somewhere amongst the household staff was a seventeen-year-old Richard Wingfield, who would come to feature prominently in Katherine's life at a later date?

The coronation of Elizabeth of York took place on 25th November 1487 and Katherine played a prominent role, perhaps hinting at her closeness to her niece. The day before the coronation, Katherine took part in a procession through the streets of London. The queen's train was carried by her sister, Cecily, and when the procession began, Cecily and the Duchess of Bedford rode together in the first carriage, directly behind the queen. That night was spent at Westminster, and the following morning Elizabeth, dressed in purple velvet, and her ladies proceeded to Westminster Abbey. The Duke of Bedford walked directly in front of the queen bareheaded in his rich robes of state, followed by the queen and Lady Cecily who again carried her train. Then came the Duchess of Bedford and other ladies, 'the Duchesses having on ther Heds Coronatts of Golde richely garnyshed with Perle and precious stones'.[13] The procession was hugely eventful it seems, with reports that amidst such huge crowds that had formed to try and cut a piece of the woollen floor covering that the queen walked on (as was the custom), a number of people were killed: 'ther was so Hoge a people inordyantly presing to cut the Ray Cloth .... in the presence certeyne Persons were slayne, and the Order of the ladies folowing the Quene was broken and distrobled'.[14] At the banquet that followed, Katherine shared the queen's table with Cecily and the Archbishop of Canterbury.

After the coronation, the couple may have again remained in London as they spent Christmas and New Year at Greenwich with the king and queen. For the occasion, Jasper had a silk dress made for Katherine at a cost of £38, 16s, 8d.[15]

Interesting snippets of the couple's daily life can be seen in surviving household accounts. We can see for two months in the year 1491, Jasper's horses were looked after at Thornbury by a Groom of the Horses, and six others, Daily meals of the duke and duchess included bread, beer, wine, mutton, pork, and salt fish.[16] From 1492 onwards, Jasper, now into his sixties, took a step back from his public duties, and most of 1494 was spent at Sudeley. The couple remained close to the king and queen and in 1494 Henry was entertained at Minster Lovell with 'ginger, oranges, conserva lymonis and mermelade'.[17]

By 1495 the couple were back at the manor house of Thornbury and Jasper was becoming seriously ill. On 15th December 1495, he drew up his will, succumbing to his illness on 21st December at the age of sixty-four. Katherine was only briefly mentioned in his will and it is likely the couple did not have a great romance. But Katherine's love story was yet to come. Following the example of her mother, in February 1496 Katherine married without licence the twenty-six-year-old Richard Wingfield, thought to be a member of her household staff. The couple were fined £20 but this was likely a small price to pay. The marriage occurred so quickly after Jasper's death, that an attraction must have been present between them beforehand. The second youngest of twelve sons, Richard was a mere knight, twelve years Katherine's junior. His elder brother, Edward Wingfield, had previously married her elder sister Jane. Having done her duty to her family and to two subsequent kings, marrying men not of her choosing, Katherine was now prepared to make her own way in life and find her own happiness.

Sadly, the couple had but a short time together, as Katherine died on 18th May 1497. She was thirty-nine years old. The couple may have remained at Thornbury, which passed into the hands of her eldest son as part of his inheritance. The ownership of Minster Lovell and Sudeley Castle reverted to the Crown on Jasper's death. They may also have made Kimbolton Castle their home, which was also a property that had been passed down through the Stafford family and the ownership of which Henry VIII gave to Richard Wingfield in 1522, and where Richard resided with his second wife and family. Richard did remarry, but he never forgot Katherine though and in his 1525 will he specified masses for Katherine's soul.

The reason for Katherine's death is not recorded, nor sadly is her burial place. Although she had given birth to four or five children during her first marriage, she produced no issue during her second to Jasper Tudor, which may be an indication of a more platonic relationship between the two? Richard and Katherine had only been married for fifteen months before her death, so it is possible that she may have died in childbirth. There is no record of a surviving child, but mother and baby may have been lost, although without any evidence this is all supposition.

Out of Katherine's surviving children, her eldest son, Edward Stafford was restored to the dukedom of Buckingham by Henry VII, and made Knight of the Garter and Lord High Constable of England, like his father.[18] He also inherited the Thornbury estates from his mother after her death. Sadly, he met the same fate as his father, rashly flaunting his royal ancestry during the reign of Henry VIII, which contributed to his execution in May 1521.

Both Anne and Elizabeth Stafford had their marriages arranged for them by their elder brother and both were in service to Katherine of Aragon. Anne was married in 1499 to Sir Walter Herbert who owned extensive properties in the Welsh Marches and was the uncle of Mary Woodville's husband, William; secondly in 1509, she married George Hastings, later Earl of Huntingdon. Anne became embroiled in a scandal when in 1510, her elder sister, Elizabeth, spoke of her concerns to her brother that Anne was developing feelings for the courtier, Sir William Compton. Whether it was Sir William who was her paramour or whether he was courting her on behalf of the king has never been firmly established, although the latter is likely. Edward surprised the couple in her chamber, immediately dispatching Anne off to a nunnery. The king was furious and ordered Katherine of Aragon to dismiss Elizabeth for her gossiping. Anne remained in favour with the king, even after her brother's execution, accompanying the court to the Field of the Cloth of Gold in 1520 and she and her husband went on to have eight children.[19]

Out of all the Woodville sisters, Katherine's life could be described as the most eventful. With four children and three marriages, her path was not so much chosen as directed by events outside of her control. Comparisons could be made to a future Sudeley resident and her namesake, Katherine Parr, with both women resolutely doing their duty to their families and their king and eventually only forging their own happiness right at the end of their lives. Both Katherines married for duty, on more than one occasion, eventually finding and choosing their own happiness before death claimed them and snatched it away before they could really enjoy it. They are both, however, brilliant examples of resilient and resourceful women of their time.

Chapter Seven

The elusive Martha Woodville

Of maidens whom he dwelt in town beside, he knew not where his fancy might abide

The final chapter in the lives of the Woodville sisters is devoted to the one whose life was so much in the shadows, there is doubt that she even existed at all. In sources referring to the Woodville family, another daughter, Martha Woodville, is often mentioned. According to these sources, Martha Woodville was married to Sir John Bromley but that is about the extent of information they give.

The Bromley family held properties and land around Acton and Nantwich in Cheshire. The elder Sir John Bromley (c.1385-1390) was reportedly one of England's greatest heroes during the reign of Henry V, taking part in many battles on French soil and eventually dying in action in 1490.[1] His son and heir was William Bromley, who married Margaret Mainwaring of Baddiley, Cheshire.

William and Margaret were parents of Sir John Bromley, who is said to have either married or have had some sort of relationship with Martha Woodville. John was born c.1430, and owing to the death of his father, William, when John was only twelve months old, his wardship was sold to Sir Randle Mainwaring, his grandfather. At the age of twenty-nine, John was knighted by Henry VI on the eve of the Battle of Blore Heath. John Bromley, however, is known to have married Joanna Hexstall, daughter of William Hexstall of Hexstall in Warwickshire. Together they had three children: Isabella, Margaret and Margery.

Several references allege that Sir John had an illicit relationship with Martha Woodville, rather than the fact that they were married. There is also much confusion over Martha's age, with her described as being possibly the youngest Woodville sibling[2] or being born as early as 1450.[3] Evidence of a perhaps an illicit relationship rather than a marriage is backed up by the existence of a son, Thomas, who was believed to be the illegitimate son of Sir John, possibly with Martha.

So, did Martha exist and if she did, was she one of the Woodville sisters? She is not mentioned at all by Robert Glover. If she was the youngest then she would surely have been born after Katherine Woodville as from Lionel Woodville born c.1453, through to Katherine's birth in 1458, Jacquetta Woodville pretty much gave birth once a year and it is highly unlikely, in the absence of Martha being a twin, that she could have been born in this period. Had she been the youngest, she would almost certainly have followed in the footsteps of Katherine Woodville and been bought up with her sister at court. No reference is found in Elizabeth's accounts for a Martha Woodville.

John Bromley was known to be a Lancastrian, he fought at Blore Heath under Lord Audley and received his knighthood and in 1471 there is reference to a Sir John Bromley serving with the garrison at Calais.[4] Calais in 1471 was filled with supporters of the Earl of Warwick and exiled Lancastrians. If Martha had been unmarried at the time Elizabeth became queen, surely a marriage would have been arranged for her and Sir John Bromley, an avid Lancastrian, seems an unlikely match.

Another possibility is that she was one of the elder girls, and that like her sister Jacquetta, her marriage was arranged before Elizabeth became queen. From 1437 to 1439, Anthony, Elizabeth and a son called Richard (who died early) were all born. There is then a five to six-year gap, when two other possible children were born (Louis and another Richard) and then John Woodville was born in 1465. Martha Woodville could have been born sometime between 1440-1445, which would have made her a similar age to John Bromley.

However, Joanna Hexstall who is known to have married Sir John Bromley, was still alive in 1470, when she and her husband sued three men for illegal entry onto their land.[5] As he already had a wife, a marriage contract between the pair pre-1465 is also looking unlikely.

A possible scenario is that Martha was one of the older Woodville girls and had some sort of illicit relationship with John Bromley that resulted in a pregnancy. Birth dates for Thomas are given as early as 1465 – he is only known to have been born by April 1478 when his father awarded him an annual rent of 20 marks. The Woodville family were also initially Lancastrian supporters – it is not beyond the realms of possibility that at some point in the early 1460s, a young Lancastrian knight, somewhere in his early twenties, visited the manor of Grafton and fell in love with a Woodville girl a couple of years his junior. As he was already married, the pair may have struck up a forbidden relationship. If, Martha was an unmarried woman, either pregnant or with an illegitimate child in 1465, it is quite likely that the Woodville family would have wanted her kept out of the limelight. She certainly would not have been considered a good catch when her sisters were found husbands and may even have found herself destined for a nunnery, as was the lot of many women who found themselves in difficulties after an illicit relationship.

Magna Brittanica: The County Palatine of Chester (Daniel Lysons) describes a pedigree in a collection belonging to a Mr Woodnoth's that mentions 'Thomas Bromley was the only son of Sir John Bromley the younger, grandson of Sir John Bromley, who distinguished himself in the wars of France, by his second wife Martha, daughter of Richard Widville, Earl Rivers'. Maybe if she did exist, and the couple were in love, she eventually become his wife after the death of his first wife, Joanna, sometime after 1470.

Thomas Bromley was known to have married and had several children. One of his younger sons, William Bromley, lived at

Dorfold Manor and, as well as being Controller for the Earl of Derby, he sat in parliament. He biography states he was 'the 6th s(on). but h(eir). of Thomas Bromley (illegit. s. of Sir John Bromley of Barthomley and 'Hextall', Cheshire).[6]

Thomas' mother, Martha, may not have been a Woodville at all, or she may not have been part of the Woodville family from Grafton. But if she was the queen's sister, she is a complete mystery, which perhaps makes her the most intriguing of them all!

Conclusion

The period we now call 'The Wars of the Roses' was a hugely troubled time in our history and the Woodville family became players on the main stage. On that day in May 1464 when Elizabeth followed her heart and married her king, she most definitely advanced her family, but she also placed them right into the heart of the political turbulence.

For all countrymen during this period, danger was commonplace. Noble families took sides against each other in support of Lancaster or York, and peasant families, who in the main probably didn't understand or even care who was in power, had to live with the reality that their men folk could be conscripted at any time by the lord of their manor and marched off into battle. For the women folk, staying home and wondering if their father, brothers, sons and husbands would return was part of their lives. This was no different for the Woodville women. The Woodville men had previously taken part in battles, fighting on the Lancastrian side, and were not closeted from danger, but after 1464 Elizabeth's proximity to the king elevated her family into becoming targets for the king's enemies.

The reason I chose to write this book on the Woodville sisters was primarily because they only ever seem to receive a mention in other historical accounts about the period and the family. That is of course largely in part because hardly any information exists about them. Elizabeth's story is documented because she achieved the high status that she did, and as a heroine of mine I am of the viewpoint that what she achieved, against all the odds, is worthy of telling. But the more I studied Elizabeth's life, it struck me that her sisters also lived through the same period, they also experienced the joy of Elizabeth's coronation, the utter sadness at the loss of their brothers, parents, and each other, and their stories are just as valid an account of the life of fifteenth century women. They did not themselves achieve queenship, but they had to live with the consequences of their sister joining the royal court and what that meant to themselves and their families.

Due to the lack of documentary evidence, the accounts of their lives understandably contain many 'likelies', 'probablies' and 'maybes'. This is unavoidable – from a distance of over five hundred years, it is impossible to know their emotions, motives or mindset and this applies to all historical figures, not just the Woodvilles. The chroniclers at the time left records of events – we know who was where and at what time because those are the facts. What we are not privy to is why people made the decisions they did, or how they felt. Therefore, a writer's view on history can only ever be speculative and depending on the perspective of the writer, it is likely always to be slightly biased, as the writer applies their own experience of life to their observations. Richard III, for instance, has his supporters and his detractors depending on which account you read – was he a loyal brother, and man of honour or was he a ruthless child murderer? Was Anne Boleyn a woman who married for love, a highly ambitious, driven woman seeking advancement, or a young girl pushed into a courtship against her wishes that ultimately led to her tragic end? Humans are extraordinarily complex, and the truth is probably that Richard III and Anne Boleyn cannot be defined by any one of those descriptions.

In researching the lives of the Woodville women, it seems that Elizabeth's sisters did, in the end, fare better than their male siblings. Out of the five Woodville brothers, none produced legitimate offspring, and only two died of natural causes. Their father and brother, John, were executed by Warwick's men. Fourteen years later, Anthony Woodville and Elizabeth's son, Richard Grey, also met a violent death when they were executed by Gloucester's men and another brother, Edward Woodville, died in battle in Brittany in 1488 (although soldiering was his chosen vocation and his death cannot be attributed to the Wars of the Roses).

All the sisters apart from Jacquetta had their marriages arranged for them, but at least two, Katherine and possibly Jane, were able to marry a man of their choosing later in life. That is not to say that the arranged marriages meant a life of unhappiness, in all probability one or two of them would have been able to achieve a happy union first time around – Margaret is a strong contender for this scenario if her husband, Thomas, was indeed a 'a tender and affectionate husband'. All the Woodville girls bore children (Jane being the one possible exception) and hopefully managed to create for themselves a stable family life amongst all the turmoil of the period they lived in.

By the 1490s, twenty-five years after Elizabeth became Queen of England, only two Woodville sisters were still living, Katherine understandably as the youngest and Elizabeth, who proved herself the greatest survivor, dying at the relatively old age of fifty-four. From her small room in the abbey in Bermondsey where she spent her last days, how much did she reflect on those early days at Grafton and how her love affair had changed her family's destiny? Her sisters may have been affected by her decision but they, like the rest of the family, managed to weave a life for themselves that have made them a part of the fabric of our history today.

Appendix One

The children of Richard Woodville and Jacquetta

Anthony Woodville. Born c.1437/38.
Married 1st Elizabeth Scales; 2nd Mary Fitzlewis.
No legitimate issue.

Richard Woodville. Born c.1438/39. Died young?

Elizabeth Woodville. Born c.1438/40. Married 1st Sir John Grey of Groby.
Issue: Thomas Grey, Richard Grey.
M. 2nd Edward IV.
Issue: Elizabeth of York, Mary of York, Cecily of York, Edward V, Margaret of York, Richard, Duke of York, Anne of York, George Plantagenet, Catherine of York, Bridget of York.

Lowys Woodville. Born c.1440-1444. Died young.

Richard Woodville. Born c.1440-1444. Unmarried.
No legitimate issue.

John Woodville. Born c.1445. Married Katherine Neville, Duchess of Norfolk.
No issue.

Jacquetta Woodville. Born c.1446. Married John Lestrange, Baron Knockyn.
Issue: Joan Lestrange.

Anne Woodville. Born c.1447. Married 1st William Bourchier.

Issue: Henry Bourchier, Cecily Bourchier, Isabel Bourchier.
M. 2nd George Grey.
Issue: Richard Grey.

Mary Woodville. Born c.1447-1451. Married William Herbert.
Issue: Elizabeth Herbert.

John Woodville. Born c.1448-1452. Died Young?

Lionel Woodville. Born c.1453. Unmarried.
No Issue.

Margaret Woodville. Born c.1454. Married Thomas Maltravers.
Issue: William Fitzalan, Margaret Fitzalan, Joan Fitzalan,
Edward Fitzalan.

Jane Woodville. Born c.1455-56. Married 1st Anthony Grey.
Issue: possibly Katherine Grey?
M. 2nd Edward Wingfield.

Edward Woodville. Born c.1456-57. Unmarried.
No Issue.

Katherine Woodville. Born c.1458. Married 1st Henry Stafford,
Duke of Buckingham.
Issue: Edward Stafford, Elizabeth Stafford, Henry Stafford,
Anne Stafford (possibly Humphrey Stafford?).
M. 2nd Jasper Tudor, Duke of Bedford.
No Issue.
M. 3rd Richard Wingfield.
No Issue:

Appendix Two

On the Woodville trail

The Cathedral and Abbey Church of St Alban, St Albans, Hertfordshire AL1 1BY. Website: www.stalbanscathedral.org

Arundel Castle, Arundel, West Sussex BN18 9AB. Website: www.arundelcastle.org

Bosworth Battlefield Heritage Centre & Country Park, Sutton Cheney, Nuneaton, Leicestershire CV13 0AD. Website: www. bosworthbattlefield.org.uk

The Castle of Brecon Hotel, Castle Square, Brecon, Powys, LD3 9DB. Website: www.breconcastle.co.uk. In 1809 part of the castle ruins and outbuildings were renovated to become one of the first 'modern' hotel in Wales.

Catherine's Cross, Ampthill, Bedford MK45 2GU. Located in the park at Ampthill, it marks the location of Ampthill Castle.

The De Grey Mausoleum, High Street, Flitton, near Ampthill, Bedfordshire, MK45 5EJ. Website: www.english-heritage.org. uk. First built in the early seventeenth century, this mausoleum contains later members of the De Grey Family. Although none of the fifteenth century De Greys are buried here, it is still worth a visit.

Grafton Regis village, Northamptonshire. St Mary's church contains the Woodville Tower and memorial tomb of John Grafton, grandfather to Elizabeth and her siblings. Grafton manor itself is now privately owned and not open to visitors but is believed to be on the site of the manor house that the Woodville's inhabited. Website: www.grafton-regis.co.uk

Minster Lovell Hall and Dovecote, Oxfordshire, OX29 0RR, Website: www.english-heritage.org.uk

Raglan Castle / Castell Rhaglan, Castle Rd, Raglan NP15 2BT. Website: www.cadw.gov.wales

Ruthin Castle, Castle Street, Ruthin, North Wales LL15 2NU. Website: www.ruthincastle.co.uk. Note: Ruthin Castle was converted into a hotel in the 1960s and in 2015 the Ruthin Castle Conservation Trust was formed, and it became a Charitable Trust. The hotel has a good section on its history on their website and holds medieval feasts in a nod to its extensive history.

St Georges Chapel, Windsor Castle, Windsor, Berkshire SL4 1NJ. Website: www.stgeorges-windsor.org. Burial place of Edward IV and Elizabeth Woodville.

St John's Church, Hillingdon. Website: stjohnshillingdon.org. uk. Home of the Lestrange brass.

Sudeley Castle, Winchcombe, Gloucestershire, GL54 5JD. Website: www.sudeleycastle.co.uk

Tintern Abbey / Abaty Tyndyrn, Tintern NP16 6SE. Website: www.cadw.gov.wales

Weobley Castle, Llanrhidian, Swansea SA3 1HB. Website: www.cadw.gov.wales

Wrest Park, Silsoe, Bedfordshire, MK45 4HR. Website: www.english-heritage.org.uk

References

Preface

1. Higginbotham, *The Woodvilles*, The History Press, 2015.
2. Ross, *Edward IV*, Yale University Press, 1997.

Chapter One

1. Le Strange, *Le Strange Records: A Chronicle of the Early Le Stranges of Norfolk and the March of Wales*, 1916.
2. *Calendar of Patent Rolls, Henry VI. PRO.*
3. Richardson, *Magna Carta Ancestry: a study in colonial and medieval families*, Genealogical Publishing Company, 2005.
4. Le Strange, *Le Strange Records: A Chronicle of the Early Le Stranges of Norfolk and the March of Wales*, 1916.
5. Ibid.
6. Leyser, *Medieval Women*, W&N, 2005.
7. Cameron, *The Brasses of Middlesex: Part 17*, Hillingdon.
8. Richardson, *Magna Carta Ancestry: a study in colonial and medieval families*, Genealogical Publishing Company, 2005.
9. Cameron, *The Brasses of Middlesex: Part 17*, Hillingdon.
10. Ibid.
11. St John's Church Hillingdon, brass leaflet. (Note: Janet and Jane are alternative spellings of Jacquetta (also documented in places as Jacinta) and Joan).
12. *A History of the County of Shropshire (Volume 2)*, Victoria County History, London, 1973.

Chapter Two

1. Myers, *Crown, Household and Parliament in Fifteenth Century England*, Continnuum-3PL, 1985. (Note Elizabeth, Lady Scales was married to Anthony Woodville.)
2. Cockayne, *The complete peerage of England, Scotland, Ireland, Great Britain and the United Kingdom, extant, extinct, or*

dormant, Volume 5, Eight Volumes, 1887-1898.

3. Baldwin, *Elizabeth Woodville, Mother of the Princes in the Tower*, Sutton Publishing, 2002.

4. Licence, *Edward IV and Elizabeth Woodville*, Amberley Publishing, 2016.

5. Baldwin, *Elizabeth Woodville, Mother of the Princes in the Tower*, David Sutton Publishing, 2002

6. Licence, *Edward IV and Elizabeth Woodville*, Amberley Publishing, 2016.

7. Bernard, 'The Tudor Nobility', Manchester University Press, 2002.

8. Harris, *English Aristocratic Women, 1450-1550: Marriage and Family, Property and Careers*, Oxford University Press, 2002.

9. Susan Higginbotham in an article for the Richard III society.

10. Richardson, *Magna Carta Ancestry: a study in colonial and medieval families*, Genealogical Publishing Company, 2005.

11. Ibid.

Chapter Three

1. Lee, *Dunster: A Castle at War*, Mereo Books, 2014.

2. Ross, *Edward IV*, Charles Yale University Press, 1997.

3. Raglan Castle, CADW, 1998.

4. Breverton, *Henry VII, the maligned Tudor King*, Amberley Publishing, 2016.

5. Richardson, *Magna Carta Ancestry: a study in colonial and medieval families*, Genealogical Publishing Company, 2005.

6. Breverton, *Henry VII, the maligned Tudor King*, Amberley Publishing, 2016.

7. Raglan Castle, CADW, 1998.

8. *Admissions Register Vol 1 1420-1799*, by the Honourable Society of Lincoln's Inn, pub. 1896.

9. Raglan Castle, CADW, 1998.

10. Breverton, *Henry VII, the maligned Tudor King*, Amberley Publishing, 2016.

11. Corbet, *Edward IV: England's Forgotten Warrior King: His Life, His People and His Legacy*, iUniverse, 2015.

12. Sutton and Visser-Fuch, *Royal Funerals of the House of York at Windsor*, Richard III Society, 2005.

13. Richardson, *Magna Carta Ancestry: a study in colonial and medieval families*, Genealogical Publishing Company, 2005.

14. Raglan Castle, CADW, 1998.

15. Sutton and Visser-Fuch, *Royal Funerals of the House of York at Windsor*, Richard III Society, 2005.

16. Robinson, *Tintern Abbey*, CADW, 2011.

Chapter Four

1. British History Online.

2. Eustace, *Arundel, Borough and Castle*, Robert Scott, London, 1922.

3. Roberts, The Institute of Archaeology Field Course at Downley Park, Singleton, West Sussex, UK. Multi period excavations around the hunting lodge of the Earls of Arundel. *Archaeology International*, 21, pp.141–152, 2018.

4. Roberts, quoting 'Nomanes Land, 15th January 4 Edward III 1331. Sharp (1908)', 2018

5. "F.M.," "Christening of the Princess Bridget, 1480." *Gentleman's Magazine*, January 1831.

6. Tierney, *The History and Antiquities of the Castle and Town of Arundel; including the biography of its Earls, from the Conquest to the Present Time*, 1834.

7. Ibid.

8. Ibid.

9. Ibid.

10. Thanks to the Craig Irving, Manager of Arundel Castle archives for this information.

11. Tierney, *The History and Antiquities of the Castle and Town of Arundel; including the biography of its Earls, from the Conquest to the Present Time*, 1834.

Chapter Five

1. Cockayne, *The complete peerage of England, Scotland, Ireland, Great Britain and the United Kingdom, extant, extinct, or dormant*, Eight Volumes, 1887-1898.
2. Jones, *The Hollow Crown: The Wars of The Roses and the Rise of the Tudors*, Faber & Faber, 2015.
3. Richardson, *Magna Carta Ancestry: a study in colonial and medieval families*, Genealogical Publishing Company, 2005.
4. Newcombe, *An account of the castle and town of Ruthin*, BiblioBazaar, 2009.
5. Gristwood, *Blood Sisters: The Women behind the Wars of the Roses*, Harper Collins, 2013.
6. Wrest Park. Research Report Series 6- 2013. WREST PARK, SILSOE, BEDFORDSHIRE LANDSCAPE INVESTIGATIONS. Magnus Alexander. With Andrew Hann, Fiona Small and Paddy O'Hara.
7. Hicks, *The Family of Richard III*, Amberley Publishing, 2015.
8. Richardson, *Magna Carta Ancestry: a study in colonial and medieval families*, Genealogical Publishing Company, 2005.
9. Austin, *History of a Bedfordshire family; being a history of the Crawleys of Nether Crawley, Stockwood, Thurleigh and Yelden in the county of Bedford*, 1911.
10. St Albans Cathedral.
11. Sutton and Visser-Fuch, *Royal Funerals of the House of York at Windsor*, Richard III Society, 2005.
12. Wilkins, *The Last Knight Errant: Sir Edward Woodville and the Age of Chivalry*, I.B. Tauris, 2016.
13. Richardson, *Magna Carta Ancestry: a study in colonial and medieval families*, Genealogical Publishing Company, 2005.
14. Campbell (ed.), *Materials for a History of the Reign of Henry VII*, Longman & Co, 1873.

Chapter Six

1. Baldwin, *Elizabeth Woodville, Mother of the Princes in the*

Tower, Sutton Publishing, 2002.

2. Myers, *Crown, Household and Parliament in Fifteenth Century England*, Continnuum-3PL, 1985.

3. Rawcliffe, *The Staffords, Earls of Stafford and Dukes of Buckingham: 1394-1521*, Cambridge University Press, 1978.

4. www.castlewales.com/brecon

5. Jones, *The Hollow Crown: The Wars of The Roses and the Rise of the Tudors*, Faber & Faber, 2015.

6. Gristwood, *Blood Sisters: The Women behind the Wars of the Roses*, Harper Collins, 2013.

7. Rawcliffe, *The Staffords, Earls of Stafford and Dukes of Buckingham: 1394-1521*, Cambridge University Press, 1978.

8. Bayani, *Jasper Tudor: Godfather of the Tudor Dynasty*, MadeGlobal Publishing, 2015.

9. Ibid.

10. Gristwood, *Blood Sisters: The Women behind the Wars of the Roses*, Harper Collins, 2013.

11. Bayani, *Jasper Tudor: Godfather of the Tudor Dynasty*, MadeGlobal Publishing, 2015.

12. Ibid.

13. Leland, *Joannis Lelandi Antiquarii de rebus Britannicis Collectanea*, Thomas Hearne, 1770.

14. Ibid.

15. Bayani, *Jasper Tudor: Godfather of the Tudor Dynasty*, MadeGlobal Publishing, 2015.

16. Ibid.

17. Ibid.

18. Rawcliffe, *The Staffords, Earls of Stafford and Dukes of Buckingham: 1394-1521*, Cambridge University Press, 1978.

19. Levin, Riehl Bertolet, and Eldridge Carney (eds.), *A Biographical Encyclopedia of Early Modern Englishwomen: Exemplary Lives and Memorable Acts 1500-1650*, Routledge, 2016.

Chapter Seven

1. Bromley, *Bromley: Midlands Family History, and the search for the Leicestershire Origins*, Matador, 2006.
2. Ibid.
3. Corbet, *Edward IV: England's Forgotten Warrior King: His Life, His People and His Legacy*, iUniverse, 2015.
4. Bromley, *Bromley: Midlands Family History, and the search for the Leicestershire Origins*, Matador, 2006.
5. Ibid.
6. History of Parliament Online

Select Bibliography

Baldwin, David, *Elizabeth Woodville, Mother of the Princes in the Tower*, Sutton Publishing, 2002.

Bayani, Debra, *Jasper Tudor: Godfather of the Tudor Dynasty*, MadeGlobal Publishing, 2015.

Dunleavy, Brian, *The Woodville Chronicle*, Magic Flute Artworks Ltd., 2017.

Gregory, Phillipa, *The Women of the Cousins War: The Real White Queen and her Rivals*, Simon & Schuster Ltd, 2013.

Gristwood, Sarah, *Blood Sisters: The Women behind the Wars of the Roses*, Harper Collins, 2013.

Harris, Barbara J., *English Aristocratic Women, 1450-1550: Marriage and Family, Property and Careers*, Oxford University Press, 2002.

Hicks, Michael, *The Family of Richard III*, Amberley Publishing, 2015.

Higginbotham, Susan, *The Woodvilles*, The History Press, 2013.

Jones, Dan, *The Hollow Crown: The Wars of the Roses and the Rise of the Tudors*, Faber & Faber, 2014.

Leyser, Henrietta, *Medieval Women: A Social History of Women in England 450-1500*, W&N, 2005.

Licence, Amy, *Edward IV and Elizabeth Woodville*, Amberley Publishing, 2016.

Licence, Amy, *Elizabeth of York – Forgotten Tudor Queen*, Amberley Publishing, 2013.

Licence, Amy, *Red Roses: Blanche of Gaunt to Margaret Beaufort*, The History Press, 2016.

Macgibbon, David, *Elizabeth Woodville – A Life: The Real Story of the White Queen*, 2013.

Weir, Alison, *Elizabeth of York: The First Tudor Queen*, Ballantine Books, 2014.

Weir, Alison, *Lancaster and York*, Vintage, 2009.

Wilkins, Christopher, *The Last Knight Errant: Sir Edward Woodville and the Age of Chivalry*, IB Tauris, 2009.

Select Bibliography

CHRONOS
BOOKS

Chronos Books is an historical non-fiction imprint. Chronos publishes real history for real people; bringing to life people, places and events in an imaginative, easy-to-digest and accessible way - histories that pass on their stories to a generation of new readers.
If you have enjoyed this book, why not tell other readers by posting a review on your preferred book site.

Recent bestsellers from Chronos Books are:

Lady Katherine Knollys
The Unacknowledged Daughter of King Henry VIII
Sarah-Beth Watkins
A comprehensive account of Katherine Knollys' questionable paternity, her previously unexplored life in the Tudor court and her intriguing relationship with Elizabeth I.
Paperback: 978-1-78279-585-8 ebook: 978-1-78279-584-1

Cromwell was Framed
Ireland 1649
Tom Reilly
Revealed: The definitive research that proves the Irish nation owes Oliver Cromwell a huge posthumous apology for wrongly convicting him of civilian atrocities in 1649.
Paperback: 978-1-78279-516-2 ebook: 978-1-78279-515-5

Why The CIA Killed JFK and Malcolm X
The Secret Drug Trade in Laos
John Koerner
A new groundbreaking work presenting evidence that the CIA silenced JFK to protect its secret drug trade in Laos.
Paperback: 978-1-78279-701-2 ebook: 978-1-78279-700-5

The Disappearing Ninth Legion
A Popular History
Mark Olly
The Disappearing Ninth Legion examines hard evidence for the foundation, development, mysterious disappearance, or possible continuation of Rome's lost Legion.
Paperback: 978-1-84694-559-5 ebook: 978-1-84694-931-9

Beaten But Not Defeated
Siegfried Moos - A German anti-Nazi who settled in Britain
Merilyn Moos
Siegi Moos, an anti-Nazi and active member of the German
Communist Party, escaped Germany in 1933 and, exiled in
Britain, sought another route to the transformation
of capitalism.
Paperback: 978-1-78279-677-0 ebook: 978-1-78279-676-3

A Schoolboy's Wartime Letters
An evacuee's life in WWII — A Personal Memoir
Geoffrey Iley
A boy writes home during WWII, revealing his own fascinating
story, full of zest for life, information and humour.
Paperback: 978-1-78279-504-9 ebook: 978-1-78279-503-2

The Life & Times of the Real Robyn Hoode
Mark Olly
A journey of discovery. The chronicles of the genuine historical
character, Robyn Hoode, and how he became one of England's
greatest legends.
Paperback: 978-1-78535-059-7 ebook: 978-1-78535-060-3

Readers of ebooks can buy or view any of these bestsellers by clicking on the live link in the title. Most titles are published in paperback and as an ebook. Paperbacks are available in traditional bookshops. Both print and ebook formats are available online.

Find more titles and sign up to our readers' newsletter at http://www.johnhuntpublishing.com/history-home

Follow us on Facebook at https://www.facebook.com/ChronosBooks

and Twitter at https://twitter.com/ChronosBooks

The Queen's Sisters

Select Bibliography

The Queen's Sisters

Select Bibliography